DEDICATION

To Bill

Christian, John and Nick

I love you with all my heart.

This being human is a guesthouse.

Every morning a new arrival.

A joy, a depression, a meanness,

Some momentary awareness comes

As an unexpected visitor.

Welcome and entertain them all

Even if they're a crowd of sorrows,

Who violently sweep your house

Empty of its furniture.

Still treat each guest honorably,

He may be clearing you out

For some new delight.

The dark thought, the shame, the malice,

Meet them at the door laughing,

And invite them in.

Be grateful for whoever comes,

Because each has been sent

As a guide from beyond.

—Rumi

FOREWORD

My teacher, a Russian Orthodox theologian, the late Alexander Schmemann, told a story to illustrate his belief in angels. Many years ago, he was on the Paris metro with his fiancée–they were very much in love. An old woman dressed in the uniform of the Salvation Army got on the train and sat near the young couple. They began whispering in Russian. "Look at that old woman! Have you seen anyone so ugly?" At the next stop, the old woman got up to leave, and as she passed the couple, she said in perfect Russian, "I wasn't always ugly!" Father Schmemann said with utter conviction, "That was an angel of God!"

Look for angels in the people around you. What if the truly human is the stranger at the door–a divine emissary, an angel — our neighbor? The guest-master at a monastery in Egypt once greeted me "as an angel of God–just in case!"

"Angel" isn't a bad image to help us greet everyone we meet–*just in case* they have something to teach us, or a message we need to hear. Without such an act of imagination, we miss the risk and the hope of being connected to others.

However we understand angels, they point to three things.

1. Life is unfathomable! D.H. Lawrence: "Now a book lives as long as it is unfathomable. Once it is fathomed... once it is known and its meaning is fixed or established, it is dead."
2. We swim in a sea with uncounted fathoms beneath us.
3. The universe is alive.

What I appreciate about the notion of angels is that God is always trying to reach us and that the universe wishes us well. It is not our enemy!

James Hillman asks: "Why is it so difficult to imagine that I am cared about, that something takes an interest in what I do, that I am perhaps protected, may even be kept alive not altogether by my own will and doing? Why do I prefer insurance to the invisible guarantees of existence? Despite this invisible caring, we prefer to imagine ourselves thrown naked into the world, utterly vulnerable and fundamentally alone."

I grew up with this belief that I had no invisible protection and still find it hard really to believe that I matter much. It is easier to accept the story of heroic self-made development than the story that you may well be loved by this guiding providence, that you are needed for what you can bring, and that you are sometimes fortuitously helped by it in situations of distress.

To say that you have a guardian angel is a way of saying you have a unique and unrepeatable role to play in the mystery of the universe and that you are watched over and protected in your vocation to be you. If you start to believe that, you will, in the power of the Spirit, be more who you are called to be—a member of the community of God, a friend of God, and an agent of peace and reconciliation in a broken world.

May God open our eyes as God opened the eyes of our forebears to see the legions of angels surrounding us. As James Hillman writes: "O Raphael, lead us toward those we are waiting for, those who are waiting for us: Raphael, Angel of happy meeting, lead us by the hand toward those we are looking for. May all our movements be guided by your light and transfigured with your joy."

The Very Reverend Alan Jones

INTRODUCTION

From a young age, I have believed in the existence of angels. Certainly no expert, I just *knew* they were *there* for me and for everyone. I see them as spiritual beings, highly conscious guides, who love us and want only the best for us. Gary Quinn explains in his wonderful book, *May the Angels Be with You*, that angels are also messengers, "the wires of the universe—they afford us a means of spiritual communication... They can be people we've loved on this earth who have passed over, or they can be spiritual beings we haven't known."

Appearing in any form God decides, they can communicate with us through a song, a fragrance, a verbal suggestion, a commanding voice or a dream. With powers and abilities far beyond ours, they lead us to a greater understanding of our own capacity to love; they also help us see how transformative the power of love can be. For me, angels can also be people—strangers, family, and friends— whose lives have touched mine in this life, whose loving actions have opened up my heart to greater love and understanding. I place animals in this category as well.

Years ago at a low point in my life, I had a powerful dream of being with angels. They were showing me paintings I had done that were hung throughout an immense room. I was particularly drawn to one on the ceiling of two angels looking downwards. Then I felt many arms cradling me as one would cradle a baby. When I awoke, I was filled with a sense of love and security. That dream gave me strength to continue, with firmer steps, on a path that was both painful and challenging.

In a recent move, I reconnected with an old friend who for many years had been a tennis partner and opponent. We delighted in our "new" friendship; we began playing bridge together and shared tennis stories and pictures of our families. One day at the bridge center, she noticed I was holding Eben Alexander's *Proof of Heaven*; taking a quick look, she turned to me and said forcefully, "Linda, how can you be *so* naïve as to think that there is anything or anybody beyond this life now?" Stunned, I said, "It's a wonderful book. You should read it." Shaking her head, she just laughed.

One week later she got the terrible news she had terminal cancer that had spread so quickly she had only weeks to live. When I went to visit, Hospice was there, and she was already going in and out of consciousness. Holding her limp hand, I started talking. "Joan, you are surrounded by love. You are not alone. You are beloved." She squeezed my hand; her eyes opened, and she smiled. "Linda, you make me feel so wonderful, so happy." Then she drifted off. I stayed with her for a long time telling her about God and angels and how she would be lifted home with love.

Two days later on a crystal clear, windless morning, I was playing tennis. My opponents were taking a break, and I was standing near the net. Suddenly, out of nowhere, a gauzy, wispy cloud appeared in front of me and stayed there for over five minutes, hovering, not dissipating. Right then I knew beyond knowing it was Joan coming to reassure me that she now understood she was in the arms of angels and that I shouldn't worry. She died the next morning.

The Love of Angels includes my own stories and those of others who have shared their encounters with loving beings. It is my hope that these stories will lift our hearts and be reminders of our connection to the Divine. The word angel means messenger in both Greek and Arabic. Aren't we all messengers, sending a message to those around us through the lives we lead? Thomas Merton wrote, "Because we love, God is present." Living our lives in love is what carries us onwards in our journey home to the light on that distant shore.

Linda Bucklin

Mill Valley, California

March 2016

MONTANA LIGHT

On my way to the Sun River, off in the distance I see huge ravens swooping and rising above the desolate plains. They are black, black as a moonless night, yet in an instant, as the afternoon sun hits their wings, they turn pale as the dry grass across which their shadows brush. How amazing! What we know to be black can be white in a different light.

I must remember this image of black and white wings. It takes me beyond what I know to be true on one level to a deeper place, enlarging my view of this precious life and reassuring me that where there is darkness, there is also light. And with the light I can see in the distance diaphanous wings of angels.

LB

MY MOTHER, MY ANGEL

Recently, I had a reading with an intuitive who knew only my first name and phone number. A few minutes into the reading, she stopped abruptly and said, "Is there anyone in your family whose name starts with "M?" I think and think. "No," I said, "no name comes to my mind." She pressed me. "Are you certain?" Anyone whose name begins with M-A-R, perhaps a Marie?" Suddenly, I knew. "Marialice," I said. "It's the formal name of my mother who died in 1969. Everyone called her Pat."

"Yes," the intuitive said, "*Yes*, your mother is here. She wants you to know she's very proud of you and the way you've raised your boys. She's telling me she had strength issues on earth, she was at her wits' end, she thought that she couldn't do anything right, that she was worthless. Even though she had children, she felt there was no other way out. She didn't want people fussing over her. She is showing me her body lying in a corner. She did this herself. But it's all healed and forgiven now between your parents. And she's forgiven herself, too. Now she is a healing soul on the other side. She's very peaceful. Don't worry." Overwhelmed by her accuracy, I started crying and couldn't stop.

She continued. "Your mother wants you to be strong because she was not. She tells me she visits you in a room on the second floor of your home, on the right side of the house as you face it from the street. That's where she feels the most comfortable. That's where she brings you light. She wants to give you a big hug and tell you how proud she is of your books. She feels she's helped you in your writing. She tells me you and your sister are the daughters she loves so much. She's handing me something she wants to give you. It's a rose."

Everything the intuitive told me rang true. At the end of my mother's life, she was beaten down by my father; she did feel as if there were nothing she could do right. She'd lost her emotional strength, devastated by his mean words and the unraveling of their marriage. Supposedly, she shot herself with my father's pistol, but there were inconsistent, puzzling details surrounding her death that made me and others wonder whether she had indeed taken her own life or whether my father had killed her. Either situation was devastating, as was not knowing what had really happened. From the reading I received a definitive, however painful, answer.

What feels accurate to me as well is my mother visiting me in my study and feeling most comfortable there. After all, for years before it became my workplace, it was the nursery, occupied first by Christian, then John and finally Nick. Several times I would sense her presence as I sat reading to them at night. My mother loved books, but more than that, she would have doted on her grandchildren. And I also know that I never could have written, *Beyond His Control,* a memoir about my difficult relationship with my father, without sensing her support.

When the healer tells me my mother wants to give me a big hug, I cry even more, because in life, while she was kind and loving, she was preoccupied as well. Many times when she would stroke my hair or touch my arm, I wished instead she would hug me strongly, holding me for minutes close to her heart. And when the healer says my mother is offering me a rose, our favorite flower, I know for certain she is an angel watching over me.

Emotionally elusive in life, despairing as she neared death, my mother now surrounds me with strength and absolute love. When I am feeling weak and uncertain, I imagine her nearby, smiling, beckoning me, and I move forward into her open arms.

Recently I had a reading with a different intuitive. At the start of the session, she notes my mother is with us. "She has lots to say to you. She's still with you, there is strong thread connecting you. It's been wonderful for her to watch you grow spiritually. She's seen your strength as you move through difficult times. And now she finds being a grandmother is a true delight."

Many times raising my three boys, I yearned to have her partake in their lives, to pass on her love of family, her passion for books, art and music. I also needed her support and wanted her to teach me to be the best possible mother. Often I would question a parenting decision I had made. Then I would recall her kind smile and soft touch and be reassured.

The intuitive continues. "Your mother is mentioning a bathtub." As the wife of a demanding Executive, mother of four children, and active in the San Francisco community, my mother was very busy. At six I figured out the best way to have her all to myself was to sit by her side as she was taking her nightly bath. Comforted by her nearness and the fragrant smell of her lemon soap, I would dip my hands into the warm water and slid my chubby fingers over her shoulders and arms. She would turn towards me and smile.

I understand more fully now that my mother has always been nearby guiding me, loving me and loving my children. I know that she will continue to follow me through my journey in this life. My heart is full.

LB

JULIE'S HOT DOG STAND

When I was a communications major at San Diego State, I booked speakers for various events at the university. After graduation, marriage, and the arrival of two young sons, my husband and I moved to Petaluma where I intended to pursue my dream of launching my own business. However, I needed to raise money to make this happen.

I decided to open a hot dog stand—Julie's Hot Dog Stand. First of all, Petaluma didn't have such a thing, and secondly my Dad had always wanted someone in our family to run a hot dog stand. My husband and two boys pitched in. Although we were struggling to make ends meet, I kept my future business goal in mind.

One day, out of nowhere, an older gentleman approached the stand. All morning we had been surrounded by customers, but when he came up, no one else was there. He said, "Everything is going to work out really well for you." Taken aback by his comment, I was also filled with a sense of peace. It was almost as if he knew me. He then sat down on a nearby bench and started to draw.

Returning, he handed me a picture of five angels. When I looked up to thank him, he had disappeared. Now I know a lot of people in Petaluma, and I had never seen him before nor have I seen him since. After this encounter, Julie's Hot Dog Stand became very successful, and I was able to raise enough capital to launch my business. I now run a national Speakers'

Bureau, booking high profile speakers for corporate events.

I told everyone in my family about this amazing encounter. I framed this picture and still look at it every day. I am convinced that the artist was an angel, encouraging me to follow my dreams—and showing me the importance of supporting others in their dreams as well.

Julie, 49, Petaluma, CA

ON WINGS OF LOVE

With her vibrant blue laughing eyes and ready smile, my wife Carol lit up any room she entered. People were immediately drawn to her loving energy and her angelic spirit. When she died, I received many letters from close friends, as well as from people around the country who had only met her once.

A spiritual seeker, Carol had numerous readings with intuitives and psychics; during one session, she was told that the hummingbird had a special significance for her, that she, like this courageous, inquisitive bird, was always moving, always giving and inspiring others.

A few years later, while shopping at Barnes and Noble, I saw a coffee table book about hummingbirds. On an impulse, I bought it for Carol. When she saw the beautiful sketches on the inside cover, she began to cry. Our two daughters, Jody and Amy, and I were moved by her reaction and her strong identification with this bird.

Soon after Carol died, I visited my cousin, a landscape architect, at her beach house in Montauk, New York. Sitting on the deck, I saw my very first live hummingbird—until then, I'd only seen them in pictures. "Oh my God," I thought. "It's Carol."

When my cousin joined me, I asked, "Do you have a lot of hummingbirds?"

"

No," she said. "I've been coming here for 25 years and have never seen a single one."

Excitedly I called my daughter Jody, the family historian, in New Jersey, and asked if she remembered the hummingbird story. "Of course," she replied. "Dad, yesterday I also saw a hummingbird for the first time in my life!"

Days later, I was visiting friends in Aspen with my daughter Amy and granddaughter Madelyn. Another hummingbird appeared. Surprised, my host explained that at 10,000 feet, there are few small birds, and that he had never seen a hummingbird at this altitude. Later, as we were walking through town, Madelyn pointed at what looked like a hummingbird perched on a planter. A man walking by said, "That little girl must be very special. That is actually a hummingbird moth, and they don't usually come out in mid-day."

The sightings continued. In Staten Island, Carol's cousin was sitting on the stoop of her family home when a hummingbird arrived and hovered for twenty minutes. In New York, I was walking with a close friend who spied a hummingbird lying motionless on the ground. She picked it up and carried it for 20 blocks until it suddenly revived and flew off to a nearby tree.

During the three years Carol was sick, I became a better person. She gave me the gift of understanding, in deeper and more profound ways, the power of love and devoted companionship. After her death, her spirit chose the hummingbird to come to me so I would know-beyond-knowing that she was there by my side, loving me, inspiring me.

From the first sighting, I have felt Carol looking out for me, reminding me of her lessons about non-judgment and compassion, her spirit coming to me on the wings of love.

Bob, 65, Boulder, CO

HEAVEN SENT

Sometimes an angel comes into our life — out of the blue — when we need help the most. With our beautiful new baby, my husband and I moved to Kansas City where he had a new job. I knew no one. One day I was in the market and struck up a conversation with a woman. It turned out we had friends in common. Our relationship blossomed. Now I had a wonderful husband, perfect baby, and Carol, a new friend.

Soon my life changed drastically. I fell, lost consciousness, and hurt my head. After many tests, I was diagnosed with a rare form of epilepsy that didn't respond to the usual drugs. Over the next six years I had seizure after seizure, never knowing when the next one would occur. I couldn't drive. I couldn't be left alone with my child, and I lived in fear of having a serious accident.

Carol, going through a painful divorce and worried about her life, stepped in and never stopped helping me. She took me to doctor after doctor; she sorted out second opinions and was constantly researching my medical condition. One day she called to say she'd heard of a doctor on the West Coast who specialized in treating this type of seizure. There was an experimental operation that had 80 percent chance of success. Carol and my husband insisted I go for it. When I awoke, they were by my side.

Two years have passed and I am seizure-free. Carol's consistent caring, her love, her being there by my side, her never making it seem a hardship for her to spend so much time with me—all these gifts I will carry with me forever. She has been an ongoing angel in my life. Her loving care has inspired me to try to be the same for others.

Janie, 33, Kansas City, MO

ANGEL DRESSED IN LIGHT

One day I began searching for some important documents in a small storage closet. Facing a major business decision, I was stressed and worried that I wouldn't be able to find the documents.

Suddenly, I saw a shimmering light radiating from the ceiling to the floor. What was the source? There was only an overhead bulb, and in the unit, there was no mirror to create any unusual reflections. Vibrant in intensity, soft green in color, it was a brilliant glow, without specific form or detail, an abstract shape, but clearly a powerful energy. I had no doubt it was an angel. Then I heard a voice, deep and comforting say, "How can I help you if you don't settle down?"

Then it was gone. I knew beyond knowing it was a divine being.

I had never met an angel until then. I had never heard a voice when no one was in the room. Not before that day, not since. But I will always remember what it was like to be in that holy presence.

The angel didn't rescue me from the problem or tell me where to find the papers. That's an important thing to remember. It reminded me that I am not alone in my struggles. I might have expected something more eloquent, more literary, or more specifically related to my problem, but the message was simple and clear: I'm the one responsible for how I respond to a challenging situation. If I get caught up in stress and fear, if I don't settle down, I won't be able to receive the support that is offered.

It was decades ago that the angel came to visit. I don't remember where I found the documents or if I found them at all. But I remember the power of that moment, and the memory brings me back to center every time. That's when I sit quietly in gratitude and release my troubled thoughts, one by one.

Marilee, 80, Santa Barbara, CA

JUST IN TIME

When our daughter Caroline married John, my husband and I went along with her decision despite our serious misgivings. An orphan, John had difficult beginnings and no strong parenting role models. Although he'd won a sport scholarship to a good university and seemed to be doing well, we felt he wasn't equipped to face the challenges of being a husband or father.

Sure enough, right after their first baby was born, John was out the door. Because Caroline was so upset, I was as well. This marriage was never going to work, and the sooner it was over, the better. A month after they separated, Caroline found out she was pregnant again. I've never been good at sitting down and talking through my feelings, but this time I did.

I expressed my disappointment and anger and was afraid for her future. After this encounter, I distanced myself and we saw little of each other during this second pregnancy. As far as I was concerned, she asked for this, and she could handle it alone. Three weeks before the baby was due, Caroline came to our summer cabin for a visit.

The morning she was to leave, her water broke. I called a doctor who said we might have enough time to get to the nearest hospital, two hours away. Just in case, I gathered some fresh sheets and a plastic cover before we tore out the door. Driving way too fast on the gravel road, my husband hit a double bump, and the hubcaps flew off. When we stopped, he discovered that the deferential was broken, and that meant we weren't getting very far.

Limping into a nearby town, we asked a friend for help. Caroline's contractions were so close that the baby would be born before long. I stripped off my friend's bedding, replacing it with our sheets. My husband called the doctor, who talked me–step by step–through the delivery. During the entire time, I was still angry with my daughter and firm in my resolve that I would have nothing to do with this child.

It was a rainy, misty day, with clouds hanging halfway down the mountains, as I laid my grandson on the bed and wrapped him in a fresh, new blanket. Suddenly, the sun broke through the heavy clouds and shone on this beautiful baby, framing him in light. My heart was in my throat. At that moment, I knew I would love this child no matter what and that I would be very involved in his life, for he was an angel the good Lord had thrown into my arms.

I love all my grandchildren, but I am closest to him. There's a deep feeling between us that's hard to describe. Many times, he has said, "Gramma, if it weren't for you, I might have made many more mistakes in my life. There were many times when I decided not to do something because I knew it would hurt you. If you hadn't always been there for me, I wouldn't be who I am today. I think of you as my guardian angel."

Mary, 75, Pinedale, WY.

MY MOTHER'S DAUGHTER

I started drinking at 14. Drinking soon became a big part of my life, and I gravitated to drinkers. When I was in college while driving drunk, I passed out at the wheel and totaled my car. I emerged without a scratch. Fortunately, no one else was hurt either.

Some time later I was again drunk and dove into what I thought was a lake. It turned out to be six inches of water. I should have been either paralyzed or dead. Again I came away unscathed.

You'd think these two incidents would have been major wake-up calls. But I paid no attention and kept on drinking. When I married, I was still able to manage my drinking. We had two beautiful boys, and while I loved being a mother, I couldn't wait to stop nursing so I could get back to drinking.

Soon I was drinking behind my husband's back. Once, at church, I got up during the service, raced home, downed four beers, and returned before the service was over. My behavior was escalating, but I learned new ways of hiding it. I switched to vodka, brushed my teeth a lot, used heavy perfume, chewed packs of cinnamon gum. But I didn't fool my mother. One day she confronted me and said, "Vanessa, I will not have these babies raised by a drunk. They don't deserve this. They're innocent, and I will do everything to get them away from you."

She and my husband insisted I get help so I went to an expensive rehab in Tampa that was run like a country club. All day long I got to talk about myself and sit by the pool in the sun. I came back with a tan and an attitude. My husband was sweet and welcoming, but within five days, I was drinking again and hiding it. For 18 months I went to AA, all the while pretending I was sober. I couldn't put 30 days together. When I went up to accept my one-month chip, I thought everyone there must have known what a phony I was.

In those days I could be the life of the party or the bitch from hell scaring my precious sons. When I was angry, they would wrap their arms around my legs, looking up at me with tears running down their cheeks. One day I noticed that my four year old was watching a video that showed me drunk and screaming. But even this tangible evidence of my out-of-control, abusive behavior didn't deter me. I rationalized my actions, convincing myself I wasn't hurting anyone.

When my husband and I went to Memphis for his yearly reunion with college friends, I had a constant buzz on but managed to conceal it. After all I was going to AA, so he trusted me. For this trip, I had bought a big bag-type purse, so I could put my vodka bottle in the bottom and pile other things on top to hide it. I had covered the bottle with two sweaters and some newspapers and books, along with my make-up kit. We got into the van, and I carefully positioned my purse on the floorboard between us. When we arrived there was the vodka bottle sitting on top of my purse. But neither of us had touched the bag.

My husband looked at me and said, "That's it." He turned around, and as we drove the three hours home, I confessed.

"You are pathetic, and you are going to lose everything," he said. "I love you, but you've just used up all your chances."

I begged my husband to let me stay the night, then went back to my sponsor and got on my knees. "Please help me. I'm scared to death. I know I can't do this alone." Finally, I was able to look at the monster in the mirror. I saw the liar, the bloated red face, the rage-filled mother, the selfish wife, and said to myself that I never want to be that person again. I went to 90 AA meetings in 90 days. I completed all the steps. I began to believe that God would help me if I just stayed with the program. I cared about what my husband, mother and children thought of me. And I never would have been able to forgive myself if I didn't get sober before my mother died from newly diagnosed cancer.

In her final weeks, I hugged her and held her tightly and said, "Mama, you don't have to worry anymore. I'm going to be OK." She smiled and said, "I know you will. I know you will." I felt she was passing out of this world just as I was waking up to life. Looking back at that moment of the vodka bottle in the car, I am positive I did not put it on the top of my purse, and my husband didn't either. I believe one of my guardian angels did.

I thank God and my guardian angels every day for the life I now have. I never dreamed I could be the wife and mother that my husband and children deserve. My grandma and father now tell me I am very much like my mother, and that's the greatest compliment anyone could ever give me. I imagine she is an angel now, surrounding me with her strength and love. I know for certain that she is proud of me.

Vanessa, 40, Jackson, MS.

LLOYD EMERSON SCOTT

I believe we have many angels surrounding us. At the most unexpected time, we will meet someone, seemingly by chance, who makes a profound impact on us. Lloyd Emerson Scott was one such person, an angel who *happened* into my life. I remember so clearly the day we met. I was sitting on the porch of the California Tennis Club when a tall, black man approached me. I noticed his gentle eyes, graying hair, the crisp, white tennis shorts that hugged his muscled black legs. He introduced himself and asked if I would like to hit some tennis balls. I accepted, and our friendship began.

At 30, I was still living on the surface. A naïve, unconscious young woman, I was just beginning to question who I was and where I was headed. I had never had a black friend before. After tennis we chatted over a beer. Lloyd, I learned, began playing tennis as a 10 year old, and at 20 he won the men's singles championship of the American Tennis Association, the black national tennis body. He won it again in 1944 and 1945.

At that time, his color made it difficult for him to find his way in the white world of tennis. Because of this he was determined to open as many doors as he could for others. Co-founding the San Francisco chapter of the National Junior Tennis League, a non-profit organization that provides tennis opportunities for underprivileged children, he spent much of his free time mentoring and coaching the young. He also was a tennis mentor for me, asking me to be his partner in matches against much better players than I, players who wouldn't have considered walking on the court with me unless Lloyd were there, too.

Our friendship went deeper than sharing a love for the game of tennis. Despite our different backgrounds—he was a black male, 22 years older, and a vice president in the trust department of Bank of America—we had common interests. We were both struggling writers. We loved books and poetry. But more than that, we yearned to understand ourselves and our role in the world. Lloyd was even working on an essay entitled "Another View of God" that stressed the importance of the search for a higher self.

One day he asked me to have lunch at Enrico's, a North Beach hangout on Broadway Street. When I arrived, I saw Charles McCabe, the *Chronicle* columnist, so I sat and chatted with him. Then Lloyd arrived, wearing an elegant pinstriped suit, a copy of *The Little Prince* under his arm, and a single red rose in his hand. For once in his life, McCabe was at a loss for words. That day Lloyd and I talked of beauty, and later he sent me a letter: "Last night I saw a new moon, standing clear and high in the sky over the ocean. I stopped my car and stood outside quietly, drinking in the presence of beauty. If you saw it, too, I'm sure you would think it beautiful. Knowing this, I am not alone."

At another lunch Lloyd shared a story about his recent business trip to New York that had upset him. Arriving on the 83rd floor of the World Trade Center to meet a business associate and carrying a package under his arm, he approached the receptionist. She was on the phone, and after a cursory glance at Lloyd, kept right on talking, gossiping with her girlfriend. Lloyd waited patiently, ready to give her the name of the man he was meeting.

Finally, exasperated, she gestured dismissively for him to put the package on her desk. "She thought I was the delivery man," he said.

Through our many conversations and by his example of love and acceptance, Lloyd enlarged my vision about what was important in life. He taught me much about the value of true friendship, about how, no matter our differences, we are all connected to each other and to God. More than anyone else at that time in my life, he opened my heart to deeper levels of understanding how to become a better friend. He was one of my angels who helped me find my way.

Once he shared with me his thoughts on friendship: He wrote: "A wise man once said that love is the finest relationship that can exist between human beings. If his statement is true, and I believe it to be so, then friendship, a facet of love, is of the same high order. In friendship one gives without thought of return; one shares one's thoughts and feelings without fear of judgment. One learns to understand these simple words: love, responsibility, respect, dignity of humankind and reverence for life."

Our friendship continued, but now with three young sons, I was busier than I had been when we first met. Several times I had to cancel a lunch or tennis date. One day I saw him, briefcase in hand, walking down Montgomery Street and ran across and gave him a big hug. "Hello stranger," he joked. "Where have you been?" We made a firm date for tennis, but then we were rained out. And then weeks later, I heard of his death. On February 4, 1982, Lloyd had taken his own life. I couldn't imagine my gentle, loving friend dying that way and for many months, I struggled to understand.

One evening, at our camp in Montana, I watched the full moon rise above the mountains, and was reminded of his goodness and grace. Today when I open a book, any book, I remember the words he so loved, "And written words were footsteps, feet running hard to another person." I walk on the tennis court and there he'll be, clear in my memory, smiling and saying, "Linda, just punch those volleys!" When I go to Grace Cathedral, I often recall what he said once, as we were leaving the service. "Let us keep our eyes heavenward lest our hearts grow cold." Now an angel, he is always with me.

LB

SHAKING MY HEAD

I never thought about angels, nor did I give them any credence, until one dark, winter evening. Leaving our duck club, I noticed my gas indicator was on. I remember saying to myself, "No problem. I have more than enough to get me to the nearest station." However, it just so happened that when I reached Marysville, I hit every green light, forgot all about my need for gas, and zoomed through town. On the freeway, there was little traffic, and I said, "At this rate, I'll be home in no time."

Fifteen miles past Marysville, I suddenly heard a loud voice say *gas.* At that moment I remembered what I had forgotten to do—get gas! Here I was on a dark, desolate freeway, no cell phone, not knowing of any gas station within 20 miles. "Oh, my God," I thought. "I don't even have enough to get back to Marysville."

At that very moment I looked up, and there on the other side of the freeway, all lit up, was a gas station. And I was nearing an off-ramp that, in all my hundreds of trips to and from the duck club, I had never noticed before. It was on the other side of the road, and easy to miss. It happened to be in the tiny town of Linda, the name of my beloved wife.

I am still shaking my head over my good fortune. I have no explanation for this voice. I am growing deaf, but it was clear as a bell. It must have come from an angel, who rescued me from a very unpleasant situation.

Bill, 80, San Francisco

BROWN LEATHER COWBOY HAT

In high school I was a waitress at a burger joint called Orbakers. I had tons of regulars, one of whom really stood out. His name was Mr. DeVoight. (His wife was my high school English teacher.) He loved basketball, and since I was the starting forward, he came to many of my games and practices. He always wore a brown leather cowboy hat, like one you'd picture on an Australian cowboy. Over time, he became a staple in my life, a supportive mentor.

I didn't know that he had been fighting cancer for the past 10 years. When he died rather suddenly, I was very upset because our last interaction had been so abrupt. I had been at work on a Friday night. The place was crowded and I was very busy. He'd come in, full of ideas and suggestions on how I could get through my senior year and into a good college. I didn't have time to talk, so I brushed him off.

A few weeks later, devastated by his death, I had a particularly rough shift at the burger joint. Working hard to finish my senior year of high school, I was overwhelmed with college application deadlines, SAT prep, and carrying my basketball team to sectionals, It was one of those hard times in life, when I had no hope that anything would ever turn out right.

Lost in thought, I looked up and caught sight of a leather cowboy hat. For a split second, I felt Mr. DeVoight's presence, and expected him to walk over to say hello. My heart stopped. I didn't actually see him, but I heard his kind, measured voice: "Take things one step at a time; slow down, don't be so hard on yourself." Then the world started moving again, I lost sight of the cowboy hat. But from that moment on, I stopped worrying and felt I could handle my life's challenges. I feel Mr. DeVoight is still watching over me, giving me wise and practical advice.

Mary, 33, San Francisco, CA

ELLIE SHARP

My friend Ellie Sharp died last year, days before her 102nd birthday, after a long life filled with family, friends, and well-fed Labradors. An expert horsewoman, skier, duck hunter, fly fisherwoman, tennis player, bridge competitor, and chef/entertainer extraordinaire, she was in always on the run. Her warm spirit, sense of humor, and inclusiveness drew people of all ages.

Soon after she took up hunting, she could outshoot most men, and in 1946, was cited by *Sports Illustrated* as the first woman "to break the barrier" and be accepted into the Flamingo Duck Club, a men's club near Marysville.

The year Ellie was 85, we were both up at Sugar Bowl, a ski resort in the Sierras. Ellie had been asked to forerun the Silver Belt Giant Slalom Masters Race, a very challenging course that wound its way down a double black diamond run. It had snowed all night; by morning a winter storm watch was in full alert. She was up early, stretching and preparing for the race. By the time she got onto the chairlift, the winds were blowing gale force, visibility was almost zero, and all the other lifts had been closed. I watched her rock back and forth as the chair inched up to the summit.

Forced to wait in freezing conditions while race officials deliberated for over an hour about whether or not to cancel the event, Ellie finally got the go-ahead, and off she went. Waiting anxiously near the bottom, I finally saw her coming, a tiny red dot skiing down the Steilhung, a steep face ringed by rocky cliffs that dropped perpendicularly down to the flats. Ellie finished the race in two minutes and fifty seconds. When I hugged her, she said, "Snow is great, but God, it's cold. I'm going to the bar for a hot toddy." Off she skied, a wisp, all five feet and 98 pounds, a bright red powder ski suit disappearing in the falling snow.

Over the years Ellie, a member of one of the best duck clubs in California, invited my husband and me to go shooting. One winter right before her 92nd birthday, we set out in the dark, awkward in our waders. My gun made a painful dent in my shoulder, as we followed Ellie towards the duck blind. As always she was leading the way.

As we came to the edge of a deep pond, I could barely discern our destination, a few hundred yards off in the middle of Adams Lake. Ski pole in one hand and her gun on her shoulder, Ellie climbed down the bank and began wading out to the blind. The farther she went, the deeper the water became, and I watched worriedly as it came right up to the top of her waders.

Gingerly, I stepped into the water, and then stopped dead in my tracks, recalling an old duck blind surrounded by potholes, a place where I'd once fallen and my waders had filled with water. I'd nearly drowned. Now I couldn't make my feet move in the slippery mud. Then I looked up and saw Ellie, with her dog, Coot, swimming nearby. Ellie's head was tilted upward toward the sky. Some ducks were flying over, faintly outlined by the first light of dawn creeping over the eastern foothills. She motioned me to hurry up; it was time to shoot. Following her, I found the courage to cross the black water.

When Ellie was in her 90s, we invited her on a five-day camping and fishing trip on the remote Smith River in Montana. Without a moment's hesitation, she accepted, thrilled to have one more adventure. "Oh, how Jim would have loved this," she said, referring to her husband. While floating down the Smith River in a rubber raft, bamboo rod in one hand and binoculars in the other, she watched an eagle circle overhead.

The life of any party, Ellie often entertained. After hosting a dinner at a local restaurant, she was driving herself home. At the entrance to the Caldecott Tunnel another car swiped her, but didn't stop. Managing to ease her car off to the shoulder of the freeway before the engine died, she then just sat there, dazed. For the first time in her life, she was scared. It was dark, cars were whizzing by in both directions and in an era before cell phones, she had no way to call for help.

A young man, dressed in an elegant white suit, appeared at her window and told her not to worry, he would take care of everything. He stayed by her side until the police arrived, and then explained to them in detail what had happened. As they were helping Ellie into the patrol car, she gratefully turned to thank her knight in shining armor, but he was no longer there. She couldn't imagine how he could just disappear. Not particularly spiritual, she later told me the only explanation was that he must have been an angel.

Ellie had an amazing 100th birthday celebration at the Orinda Country Club. A year later she fell but was soon strong enough to accept the California Waterfowl Association's Artemis Award. As she neared her 102nd birthday she came up to her beloved duck club for the opening luncheon, looking wonderful in a hot pink warm up suit.

Preoccupied with problems of my own, I didn't see Ellie as often as I used to. Every day on my 'To Do' list, I would write "Call Ellie." Days passed, and I didn't. One Saturday I came home from duck hunting and resolved to call her the next morning. As I was about to fall asleep, the phone rang; it was Raul, Ellie's driver, telling me that Ellie had just died.

I was devastated, not only by the news but also by my absence in her final months. She had stepped in many times as a mentor, and helped cope with the loss of my mother. She had filled my life with laughter and friendship, and I had not been there for her at the end of her life.

One night Ellie came to me in a dream—looking young and radiant, and surrounded by a bright light. Holding out her arms and calling me the name she often used, Ellie said, "Angel, I'm fine. I'm so happy. Don't worry anymore." When I woke up, my heart didn't ache as much and I felt a sense of peace.

Ellie, an angel in my life, continues to inspire me to face life courageously, to embrace its opportunities, not its limits, and live with a generous heart. One of my favorite images of Ellie is from our Montana fishing trip. It's late afternoon and she's on her way down to the river. Wearing a pink bathing suit, she floats on her back, watching the swallows swoop down and skim across the water. She knows it's that special time of day when you can see the crimson cliffs clearly reflected in the smooth eddies of the river.

LB

IN THE ARMS OF ANGELS

When I was a little girl, my mother told me wonderful stories about angels. She would always add that when we pass on, we become angels taking care of those we have loved in our life on earth, showing up at the time they need us most. She'd remind me of this every night, as she kissed me and tucked me tightly into bed.

A strong, independent woman who spoke her mind, my mother made it clear to everyone how important her children were to her. A stay-at-home mother involved in every part of my childhood, my Mom was a constant, loving presence in our lives, a spiritual compass for our entire family.

When I was 21, she was diagnosed with a malignant brain tumor. Weakening quickly, she was barely able to muster enough energy to show me she recognized me. When she died in August, only six months later, we were devastated. The following Friday my Dad drove me to Washington, D.C. where I was to start my new job at the State Department. As a Presidential Management Fellow, I was placed in the Bureau of Diplomatic Security, working on cyber security issues. During this time I never slowed down long enough to process the loss of my beloved mother. Instead I pushed the grief deep down inside me, working nonstop, and only went back to my apartment to shower and sleep.

Although I appeared strong to others, keeping up this façade took a tremendous toll. The hardest time for me was when I was alone in the car, driving home from work. One night images of my mother flashed through my mind, each picture bringing a fresh wave of grief, and I lost it. Crying non-stop, I knew I was headed for a complete meltdown.

Suddenly the radio played the Sarah MacLaughlin song, *You're in the Arms of Angels*. I felt my mother nearby. Then I heard her words of advice. "Cari, allow yourself a full minute to compose yourself. Pause and breathe. Then get on with it." Next, I remembered what her mother, my grandmother June, often said, "Take a minute to put on some red lipstick; then get on with it!" Immediately I calmed down.

Often during this lonely and very painful time *You're in the Arms of Angels* would come on the radio, and I would feel reassured, sensing that my Mom was nearby, guiding me. I believe—

without reservation—that loved ones do come back to us as angels, just as my mother used to tell me so long ago, to strengthen, comfort and help us in our times of need.

Cari, 33, San Francisco, CA

FLEETING ANGELS

There have been many times in my life when angels have appeared, given me a wonderful gift, and then disappeared. In 1992, when my husband, son and I moved to San Francisco, I knew no one. Leslie, our real estate agent, had been recommended by a friend in New York. After she found us the perfect house to rent, she very kindly invited me to lunch "to meet a few locals."

One of the women on the guest list was feeling overwhelmed by family difficulties, leaving her little time and energy to attend to the friends she already had. Reluctantly, she attended, and we found that we shared a love of books, writing, and deep conversations. Eventually, we co-authored *Come Rain or Come Shine*, a book on women's friendships, and have traveled together in friendship ever since. While I have lost touch with Leslie, I am forever grateful to her, my real estate angel, for introducing me to Linda, one of the most important people in my life.

Another example of a fleeting angel was someone who shared an insight that changed my life. I was at Grace Cathedral, having walked the Labyrinth, and a priest I'd never seen before came up to me. She started talking about how marriage is a triangle involving three — husband, wife, and God.

At that time I was separated from my husband and wondering whether we should go through with a divorce. This priest's wisdom, offered to out-of-the-blue, resonated deeply and helped me understand the root of the loneliness I was feeling in my marriage because of our differing views on spirituality.

Although I never saw her again nor have I ever come across this idea of marriage being a triangle elsewhere, I have never forgotten the idea, and I took her wise words to heart. Now, years later, I am in that very triangle marriage, and the truth of this fleeting angel's words wakes me with a smile every day.

Mary, 60, Santa Cruz, CA

HEAVENLY MESSAGE

My husband and I were separated but ambivalent about where we were headed. Should we stay together or not? One of our shared joys during this difficult period was sailing, so one Sunday we took our friend's boat out for a sail. I was at the helm on a tack facing westward, and my husband was sound asleep on the deck. The time was bittersweet: I remember feeling so blessed to live in such a lovely place, but I was also feeling sad, wondering what to do about our marriage.

As I was taking in the sights around me through tears, I heard a distinct male voice say, "I didn't bring you here for you not to be all you can be." I looked around, half expecting to see someone, but there was only my husband napping. I somehow felt as if God—or an angel—were giving me much-needed advice on a painful situation.

That voice led me to realize I was feeling silenced, both spiritually and creatively, in my marriage, and that I wasn't being true to myself. Because of this heavenly intervention, I eventually gathered my courage, said goodbye, and stepped into a new, more creative and more openly spiritual life.

Lisa 50, Tacoma, WA

BRIEF ENCOUNTER

Shortly before my mother died in her late eighties, she told me this story, which took place in New York City in about 1943. A young woman in her early twenties working in personnel for a munitions plant, my mother returned late one evening from an opera at her beloved Met to her residential hotel. She emerged from the subway at 23rd and Lexington to pouring rain.

Suddenly, she felt a presence at her side, and a man with a deep voice politely said, "I'll walk you home. Please share my umbrella." My mother, though ill at ease, thought it would be rude to refuse so she walked with this stranger. Shy and nervous, she never dared look at him. They spoke very little.

When they got to her hotel, my mother gathered all her courage to look up at him and thank him. "Andrew," she told me, "one minute he was by my side and then suddenly he was gone. But I do know for certain that he was as black as the ace of spades." Here was my mother, who'd grown up in a small all-white town in central New York State, realizing she'd walked home late at night with a black man. This incident turned her into a civil rights activist.

When we were living in the Washington, DC suburbs in the sixties, my mother abruptly rose from the dinner table one evening and announced she was going to drive into the city to attend a large civil rights demonstration where Martin Luther King was going to speak. She parked in a run-down area of the city. As she was walking to the demonstration, a very tall white man appeared at her side and said, "Please take my arm; this is not a safe place for a woman alone." She gratefully accepted and this time, looked her companion in the eye. It was Bishop Paul Moore from St. John the Divine Church in New York.

These two brief encounters—profound reminders to my mother of the importance of kindness—led her to believe in angels and to know they come in different colors.

Andrew, 60, Washington, DC

CHRISTMAS ANGELS

At a recent Christmas party, I ran into Joan, a friend I hadn't seen for over a year. She had just heard of my husband's diagnosis of early onset Alzheimer's, a situation we'd been struggling with for two years and were still reluctant to talk about. I didn't know anyone our age (late 40's) who had to deal with this. It was such a painful, difficult time and I couldn't begin to tell other people what we were going through.

"I've just heard the sad news about your husband. I can't even begin to imagine how terrible this must be for you," Joan said, embracing me. Despite my efforts to keep up a brave front, I began to cry. She hugged me harder and said, "I'm going to put you in touch with a friend of mine whose husband also has the same disease."

The very next morning Joan arranged for me to talk with her friend, Elizabeth. We had a long conversation, and I felt–for the first time since my husband got sick—that I was not alone. Elizabeth was the first person I had spoken with who truly understood. I was in a puddle of tears after we rang off. Finally a sympathetic voice! Someone who really gets it! I thanked Joan a thousand times over for getting us together, noting that she and Elizabeth were my Christmas angels.

Clare, 49, Napa, CA

ANGEL IN A MAROON SEDAN

Thanks to an angel in a maroon sedan, I got the Christmas Spirit. After getting gas, I put my wallet on the trunk of my car while I screwed on the gas cap. Promptly forgetting about my wallet, I jumped into my car, then turned west toward Palm Springs. An angel, however, had taken notice.

Just after the turn, I became aware of a maroon sedan. First, it was next to me, and then it fell behind and pulled over to the side. I remember noting the driver's sudden maneuver but thought nothing more about it.

At Trader Joe's, I stopped at a red light and glanced into my pocketbook. I didn't see my orange wallet. Before I could even get nervous, I looked to my left. The maroon sedan had pulled up next to me in the left turn lane, its driver leaning towards me, waving and holding something orange. My jaw dropped in amazement.

We pulled off to the side and hopped out of our cars. A woman explained she'd seen something orange on my trunk, realized it was a wallet, and had been trying to get my attention since we left the gas station. The wallet flew off the car, she swerved to pick it up and then lost sight of me.

As I looked into her lovely, kind eyes, I knew she was an angelic messenger reminding me to slow down and stay present during this busy time of year. I also saw myself in her because I knew I would have done the same. It's always wonderful to be reminded of our goodness. This is what the Christmas spirit is about—to be reminded that angels are alive and well—even here in the California desert.

Diana, 52, Palm Springs, CA

UPSTAIRS/DOWNSTAIRS

When I was pregnant with my first child, my husband and I moved to Buffalo, New York. We were looking for places to rent but weren't having much luck, as a couple expecting a baby was not a landlord's first choice. One afternoon, driving down a charming street, I said to my husband, "This is exactly where I want to live." At that moment I spotted a "for rent" sign on an apartment. We knocked and Lucy, an attractive pregnant woman about my age, answered. She and her husband owned the building; they lived in the upstairs flat and were renting out the downstairs. She welcomed us in, and we signed the lease that day. Excited about becoming new mothers at the same time, Lucy and I became instant friends.

Three weeks later I gave birth to my first child, a daughter named Keller, who was born with Down's syndrome. Lucy had a degree in special education and was incredibly loving and supportive. She helped me through those first confusing days. Then one month later, Lucy went into labor and gave birth to her first child, Michael, who also had Down's syndrome. While we had become close friends before this, because we now both had babies with special needs, our friendship became an unbreakable bond.

We remodeled the backstairs, creating easy access between our two flats. We shared a baby monitor so we could cover for one another. We shopped for groceries and cooked for each other. When Lucy returned to teaching, I watched Michael. Early on we found that when you have a child with a disability, you cannot survive without a sense of humor. We learned to laugh together.

In time, we both bought single homes. Now instead of upstairs/downstairs, we live across the street from one another. We had our second children at the same time, and Keller and Michael, now fifteen, continue to be best friends. Lucy and I became advocates for the integration of special children into mainstream education. Together, we initiated the pilot program for inclusion of children with special needs into the Buffalo school system.

As parents of children with special needs, we both have given many talks, to medical students and educational professionals, showing them the parents' perspective. We want people to understand that we all need each other and that each of us has something to offer. Just because a child is different doesn't mean he or she is not valuable. We learn from those differences. Keller and Michael have made us much more aware of that and of what is really meaningful in life.

Lucy and I have accomplished what we have because we have each other and our families. And we also thank God for bringing us together—and for giving us these extraordinary angels—our children. We believe our friendship happened because God reached out and clasped our hands together when I knocked on her door many years ago.

Charlotte, 43, Buffalo, NY

I'M SO COLD

Until the day my mother died, I had never believed in anything I couldn't touch, see or prove logically. That night, after locking up the entire house and turning on the alarm system, I went to bed, exhausted from the funeral. I fell asleep with the light on. Suddenly I felt the pressure of someone sitting on my bed. I opened my eyes and saw my mother perched there by my side.

I was stunned. Before I could say a word, my mother, shivered and said, "Pat, I'm so cold, I'm freezing." Without thinking, I hugged her and replied, "Mother, that's because you were always so cold to everyone in your life." Barely were the words out of my mouth when my mother disappeared. I sat there, silent and sad. I'd been given an opportunity to feel closer to my mother, and I wished I had responded more compassionately. But her brief bedside visit had a profound impact on me.

Before this, I had never believed in life after death; afterwards, I did. This incident also changed the way I related to everyone around me. My heart just seemed to become wide open with love. I reached out wholeheartedly to my family and friends. As I became more loving, I was able to forgive my mother for being so emotionally remote, a pattern I realized I had been following until her visit. I believe my mother was an angel returning to teach me some very important lessons that I needed to learn.

Pat, 68, Washington, DC

A FAITHFUL ANGEL

Raised to achieve and accomplish things on my own, I found it hard to show weakness in any way. Until I met Katie most of my friendships were what I would call surface ones, involving activities, ideas, children, but rarely feelings. I thought I needed to keep up appearances. Katie, on the other hand, would ask for help, whether it was watching her son after school or running some errand for her. I remember being happy to oblige but also relieved that I didn't have to ask for any favors in return. After all, I could do everything myself.

Our friendship progressed, and one day Katie said she wished I'd ask for her assistance. She felt lonely because I didn't. I realized then that my holding back was my way of being afraid to admit I was vulnerable and less than perfect, and that close friendships involve sharing both our strengths and our weaknesses. Over time, I began asking Katie for advice—about friendships I was grappling with or parenting concerns I had. The more I dared reveal my hurts and fears (along with my hopes and dreams), the deeper our connection became.

Katie also introduced me to the term "balcony people," meaning friends who sit in the audience and clap for our successes, encouraging us to become who we are meant to be in this life. She showed me that one of the best ways to be a friend is to celebrate each other in this way. Acknowledging a friend's talent, we are lifted up as well. As Nelson Mandela once said, "There is nothing enlightened about shrinking so that other people won't feel insecure around you. As we let our own light shine, we unconsciously give other people permission to do the same. We cannot hold a torch to light another person's path without brightening our own."

An ongoing angel in my life, Katie is a reminder of how to be loving and kind. One afternoon, we were having tea talking about our belief in angels. I asked if her beloved mother, who had died recently, had communicated with her. Tears in her eyes, she said "No, not yet. And I still miss her so much, especially now at Christmas. I'm having a hard time coping emotionally."

A few days later she called. I could hear her joyous energy. "After our conversation, I was making biscuits from a favorite southern recipe of my mother's. I was alone in my kitchen, and suddenly I saw my mother by my side. We talked and talked. I kept making more biscuits — eight batches in all — because I wanted her to stay. She told me to give one batch to a close friend of hers, she told me to call several of her friends, and tell them that she was at peace and happy."

Katie continued, "She came to comfort me and let me know she would always be nearby. I felt surrounded by her love."

LB

SPREAD YOUR LOVE

Not long ago I was moved by a gesture of love at the airport. I was leaving Portland, Oregon, to fly to Los Angeles. Because of stormy weather, most flights were delayed, and some were canceled. The airport was crowded with unhappy travelers, so I was delighted that for some reason my flight was scheduled to leave on time. As they announced the final boarding, I noticed a harried man running up to the counter with his briefcase in one hand and his ticket in the other. The ticket agent said that unfortunately his reservation had been cleared and his seat given away. She told him politely and kindly that she would do everything she could to get him on a later flight.

Everyone in the terminal could hear the din of his frustration. He had an important meeting in Los Angeles, and he had to get there. I couldn't help but feel for him, because I've been in similar situations where I couldn't afford to miss a flight, but everybody felt sorry for the ticket agent.

All of a sudden, a woman in her seventies walked up to this man and said that she wasn't in a hurry. She would be happy to give him her seat. As you can imagine, the man stopped right in his tracks. He looked as if he were about to cry. He apologized to her, to the ticket agent, and to everyone around for his behavior and thanked the woman for being an angel in his life. He boarded the flight smiling, relieved, and much wiser! What a blessing for the lovely woman, too. The airline got her on another flight just three hours later and also gave her a free, first-class ticket to any destination served by the company. So she was truly twice blessed.

As Mother Teresa once said, "Spread your love everywhere you go." Walk the path of love and kindness, and joy will be your constant companion.

Susan, 50, Los Angeles, CA

THE WORK OF ANGELS

Some years ago I was on a publicity tour. My friend Helen accompanied me to a radio station for a midnight interview. Afterward we walked to my car, only to discover that it wouldn't start. I lifted the hood to see if anything looked out of the ordinary. We weren't in the best area of town and we were blocks from a telephone. It was cold and beginning to rain. I told Helen that we needed an angel to help us out of this dilemma.

As we were getting back into the car, a cab driver stopped and asked if we needed any help. Helen whispered to me to have faith, even though he didn't look like the angel she expected. The drive looked under the hood and checked the battery. It was out of water. He had a jug of water in his cab and filled the reservoirs. Then he told us an interesting story. At the end of his shift, he had dropped off a passenger several blocks away and was heading home, when something guided him to take a different route. He thought it was odd but followed his intuition. Then he saw us looking under the hood and wondered if we needed help.

When we told him that he was an angel we had asked for, his delighted smile warmed our hearts. He followed us in his cab all the way back to my home, to make sure the car didn't stall, then said goodbye.

The next day I found a book about angels on my doorstep with no note. Helen and I both knew who left it.

Were these random acts of kindness, or were they specifically the work of angels? I don't believe it matters, because they blessed us, and they blessed our "angelic" cab driver. William Penn once wrote, "If there is any kindness I can show or any good thing I can do to any fellow being, let me do it now, and not deter or neglect it, as I shall not pass this way again."

Susan, 50, Los Angeles, CA

MY YEAR OF POLO

Knowing my love of riding, a friend suggested I visit an Argentine rancher who owns, raises, and trains polo ponies north of Buenos Aires. When I arrived, Nicolas, the owner's son, put me on one of their ponies and realized I was at home in the saddle. Impressed that a *middle-aged woman* could handle a horse so well, he then asked if I wanted to try hitting a ball. Intrigued, I nodded enthusiastically. After a few tries, I remember thinking, "Wow, this is fun!"

Argentines are very macho, especially in the conservative polo society, and although upper class women there do ride, no one my age has ever played polo. When I asked Nicolas if he would teach me, his father Juan protested loudly. "Women should *not* play polo. This will never work." At the end of my visit, however, Nicolas took me aside and whispered that if I ever returned to this part of the world, he would be happy to give me some lessons. Right then, I knew I was in the company of an angel.

A few months after I got home, my beloved horse died; I was distraught, and on an impulse decided to take Nicolas up on his offer. Argentine women in their 20s were now joining the game, so Nicolas could find me a saddle and lightweight mallets that fit. For four days, he gave me intensive lessons. Every few months, I flew back for more instruction, and by the end of the year I had improved considerably.

During this last visit, Juan saw me practice. Astounded that a 55-year-old woman could play at all, he was impressed with my skills. He immediately took over my training; soon I could gallop and hit the ball with a full swing into the goal. Hanging off the saddle, often I could hit from underneath the horse or behind it.

He then did something so unexpected that I was blindsided: He invited me to play on an all-male polo team. All the men are or were professionals, and their average age was 30. He also put me at first position, so I could make goals. In my wildest dreams, I never imagined I would be welcomed into this traditional, male-dominated world. Nor did I think I would be skilled enough to join a team of this caliber. I am the only woman and by far the oldest member.

I've learned it doesn't matter if you are from different countries, different generations, or speak a different language, or come from a different background. We are all connected; we share common ground. Equally important, I now believe in angels. With their generous embrace, Nicolas, said "yes," despite his father's reluctance, and Juan enthusiastically continued my training. This experience has enlarged my view of the world and made me believe that anything is possible.

Margaret, 55, Palo Alto, CA

SACRED WORDS

Winter in Sonoma. As the storm approaches, the sky is a mottled like a bruise. While I'm securing the furniture on the patio, the phone starts ringing off the hook. Mercy, a visiting nurse, has found my mother collapsed on the kitchen floor and is taking her to the hospital. I must get there right away.

After driving through a heavy downpour, I board a cross-country flight to Newark, arriving at a small New Jersey hospital in the middle of the night. A frail, withered woman shivers under a threadbare hospital sheet.

Mother has lost so much weight I barely recognize her. An orderly transfers her to a gurney then wheels her downstairs for an MRI. There is nothing more to do but wait.

I'm tired, lonely, and have been struggling to find work in California while taking care of mother's needs. So far, we've been through a stroke, a triple bypass, and major back surgery, and countless medical emergencies—all requiring last minute flights back home. Yet the hardest thing has been dealing with her dark depression. Obsessed with each calamity on the evening news, mother leaves me a string of frantic messages every week:

"Were you on that Amtrak train that got derailed?"

"Did you hear about that tourist murder in the Tenderloin?"

"Did you feel that earthquake in Sonoma?"

"Did you see that awful accident on the Golden Gate bridge?"

In the morning, the news from the doctor isn't good. The MRI shows pancreatic cancer in its final stage—yet mother seems relieved, as if this is the big disaster she's been waiting for. Relieved of her forebodings, she undergoes a full-scale personality change. Gone is the fearful anxious worrier. As Mother accepts the inevitable, she finally relaxes and starts to talk about her life.

As she shares her memories, I realize she was quite the rebel in her youth. When she worked at an aircraft plant during WW II, and management wanted to cut back on the inspections. Mother led a protest, "Our boys are facing enough danger," she said. "We can at least make sure their planes are safe to fly!" She was in love, she confessed, with a dreamy pilot named Bill who met with my father and begged him to give a divorce. "I wonder where Bill is now," she said. When she was young, my mother nurtured many hopes: she longed to become a trial attorney, a Country Western singer, and a women's hockey coach!

As mother's tumor blossoms, so does our relationship. We spend hours looking at old photographs, as she shares these hidden portions of her life. This woman has starch in her backbone and so much to teach me, I can't get enough of her. For a while, the color comes back into her cheeks, and she looks vibrant, strong, as if she might even beat her cancer.

One morning I arrive and find her very pale, and barely breathing. She's clearly taken a turn for the worse. I climb into bed and spoon her, and murmur softly in her ear, "You've done a good job here. Now you can go on to the next adventure. Do some those things you couldn't fit in, this time around."

Back in California, I'm stunned by how much I miss her. One night, I wake in the middle of the night, feel a soft breath in my ear, and know that mother has come to tell me something. I hear her say distinctly: *Sacred Words*. After mulling this phase over for a few days, I realize she has given me an assignment—to create a place where women talk about their hopes and dreams and give each other courage and support. Our recent conversations have been the template for the work she's calling me to do.

With divine intervention, things come together very quickly. In four months, I put together a nonprofit organization and secure a major grant. My board members, real life angels, hold fundraisers and spread the word about our services. That year, Sacred Words: A Center for Healing Stories is born. Women come from all walks of life—artists, writers, therapists, ministers, medical professionals, activists and fundraisers — to provide "good mothering" for one another. They tell their stories, exploring their own passion and resilience. Then they take that gumption out into the world and pass it on.

Today I'm launching a seminar on Late Blooming for women over 60 because mother showed me, in her final days, that it's never too late to grow and change. Now, before I go to sleep, I give thanks for my guiding angel who taught me to believe in eleventh hour miracles and last minute saves.

Valerie, 66, Mill Valley, CA

MARY JUNE'S TRANSFORMATION

I was skating along the Santa Monica Bay, one of my favorite spots, caught up in the fluid motion of my body when I hit a gigantic rock— actually it was only a quarter-sized stone. It caught a wheel of my in-line skate and down I went, slamming into the cement. The only one to see my less-than-graceful descent was a woman sitting on a bench. She immediately came over to make sure I was okay. Her gentle kindness and amiable countenance comforted me. She helped me to the bench, where I removed my helmet and saw that it had jagged lacerations from my skid. I was grateful that I had worn protection and that nothing was broken—just a few minor scratches and abrasions on my arms and legs.

As I got myself under control, I focused my attention on the sympathetic woman by my side. Her swollen, bloodshot eyes were a dead giveaway that she'd been crying. Feeling I could help, I invited her to have lunch with me.

We all have difficult and sometimes heartbreaking stories to tell, and Mary June (MJ) was no exception. Over a three-hour lunch I learned that her two children had been killed by a drunk driver less than a year before. Her husband was having an affair with his assistant, twenty-five years his junior, and served her with divorce papers, only weeks after she was diagnosed with breast cancer. A couple of days ago, she had been let go from her job because of all the time she missed from work for her medical care.

Through all the twists and turns of her recent life, MJ had kept remarkably optimistic, determined to rise above her challenges and hold onto a childlike trust and belief that there had to be some divine order to it all. Only minutes before my fall, sadness had overcome her and she was grieving the loss of her family and husband, her breast, her job, and the normal life she had a year before. It would have been easy to see herself as a victim and sink into despair, but MJ believed there was another, better way.

MJ had enough money to live for a few months without needing to work. Her goal now was to create a healthy, balanced lifestyle and find ways to nurture her body, mind, and spirit. She told me that she wanted to lose weight and get back into shape, simplify the clutter in her house and beautify her surroundings, learn to meditate, plant a garden, and find some good books to read to nurture her new holistic lifestyle, but she didn't know where to start.

At that moment I discovered why my angels had made me fall at her feet. When I told her about my passion for motivating others to live their highest vision and added that I was giving a three-hour workshop that evening on "Celebrate Life: Rejuvenate Body, Mind, and Spirit with Empowering Disciplines," we both laughed until we cried. What a providential encounter, and what a powerful lesson for both of us that we're always in the right place at the right time and are constantly being guided and cared for by a loving Presence. Only minutes before I crashed into her world, she was asking God for the right direction to take and the best person to guide her in living a more healthy, balanced life.

Over the next three months, I was MJ's holistic lifestyle coach. We started by writing out her goals and dreams and creating affirmations to support her highest vision for herself. She immediately implemented a well-rounded exercise regime, which included aerobics, strength training, and flexibility exercises. We tackled her kitchen, nearly emptying the cupboards, pantry, and refrigerator, then went shopping at the local health food store and the supermarket for healthy foods.

Next, we cleaned out every drawer and closet in her home, adding cheerful shelf paper here and there, and brightened some walls with new paint. We extended the theme of brightening creating two lovely gardens in a yard, where nothing but weeds had grown. Finally, I taught MJ how to meditate, a discipline that she took to like a butterfly to buddleia (a butterfly-loving plant).

MJ made a conscious choice to surrender her life to a higher power and commit herself to being the best she could be. Within six months, she was down to her ideal weight, having lost thirty-three pounds, and was fitter and healthier than she had ever been in her life. After taking a few classes in interior design, a dream of hers since she was young, she started working part-time as an assistant to a prominent designer in Santa Monica. Because of her courage and assiduity, her healthy diet, a positive and balanced lifestyle that nurtures her body, mind, and spirit, and a support team of doctors and friends, MJ feels confident that neither cancer nor any other degenerative disease will ever be part of her life again. And when she least expected it, as she was working out in the gym, she met a loving, upstanding man who shares many of her interests and has asked her to go with him on a long trip to Europe.

I have no doubt that our meeting was divinely guided for our mutual empowerment. I helped transform and enhance her life; MJ profoundly inspired and motivated me with her integrity, willing spirit, and devotion to making her life better. She realized that "if it's to be, it's up to me" and took responsibility for her own happiness and fulfillment. She has discovered her purpose, followed her heart, and begun living with authentic power and passion. MJ and I both learned firsthand that breakthroughs and miracles occur when we're willing to live our highest vision and commitment.

Susan, 50, Los Angeles, CA

MY CHANCE AT A
SECOND SERVE

I had just won my match in the finals of the Phoenix Open Tennis Tournament and was feeling pretty good. Driving home, I felt a little stiffness in my right arm and wondered if I had thrown it out on a serve. I had a lot of yard work planned and was hoping it would loosen up.

On the freeway, I felt a sudden, sharp pain in my chest, shooting across my lungs. As I entered a tunnel, I felt clammy, sweaty and lightheaded, and knew I needed to get to a hospital pretty quick.

There was a medical center at the next exit, but as I pulled up to the traffic light I must have blacked out. An angel on my shoulder woke me up, and I realized I was in no condition to be driving. When I looked up, I saw a Walgreen's drug store and headed there for help.

I managed to park and walk up to the counter and asked the clerk to call 911; then I went back to my car to lie down. Though the clerk was new to the job, she did everything perfectly, alerting her manager who summoned the paramedics. He then came and sat with me until the ambulance pulled up. I felt better as soon as I got an IV, an oxygen mask and some nitroglycerin under my tongue, but they weren't taking any chances. I was wheeled to the cardiac catheterization lab for tests. There I met Dr. Nathan Lauder, who knew many of my friends on the pro tennis circuit and had even treated the father of Billie

Jean King. It was incredibly reassuring to see his face.

Dr. Lauder found a serious blood clot blocking the main coronary artery. Immediately, he went to work and put in a stent in the arterial wall, restoring normal blood flow and saving me from a massive heart attack.

My wife and son were at my side as I recuperated in the ICU, and almost every friend who sent a card said, "You're the last person in the world we'd ever expect to have a heart attack!"

Thanks to my guardian angel waking me up, guiding me to the drugstore, leading me to the expert Dr. Lauder, I got my chance at a second serve. I know God was with me, every step of the way, making sure everything turned out right.

Brian, 68, Chandler, AZ

I AM MY OWN MIRACLE

D o angels exist? Yes.

Have I ever seen one? Yes.

What was it like? Watching Sean Penn in movie, "*Milk,*" I just knew I was in the presence of something special. Like when an impossibly high note is hit and held by a gospel singer or a painting recaptures a childhood dreamland. In that moment, the door of possibility doesn't just crack; it swings wide open.

There are all kinds of angels pilgrimaging on our planet. Each of us has the capacity and ability to be an angel in another's life. Anytime our focus is on someone else and our intention is to help, we literally become an instrument of the divine. God works Her/His grace and mercy through us. I've been on the receiving end of this love many times, whether it's the kind stranger who holds a door or the nurse whose bedside manner means more than morphine. Angels materialize anywhere and everywhere.

While in Jerusalem at the age of 30, I found myself in a café at 10 P.M. Leaving my hotel room, I listened to an inner voice that insisted: *Go.* I walked into the cafe, found a seat at the bar, when suddenly an older man, at once ancient and childlike, arrived and sat one stool over. He had soft-looking white hair, olive skin and eyes a deep ocean blue. He radiated a serenity and joy I recognized but had seldom experienced. He looked so familiar.

"Hello," I said.

"Hello," he smiled.

"Do I... know you?" I wanted to ask.

"Yes." He answered before I'd finished my sentence.

"I'm Ashley."

"I know." He nodded with tenderness.

"What's your name?" I asked, offering my hand.

"Moses," he replied.

We proceeded to sit and share that space for a bit. This may sound strange, but I didn't feel compelled to talk. I just wanted to sit by him. Words are unnecessary in the presence of an angel.

Though baptized, I had not been raised with

religion. Meeting Moses was the beginning of a deep and powerful mystical revelation. For the next few days in Israel, I stopped eating and sleeping, and the entire world cracked open like a cosmic egg. Every moment was illumined by deep meaning and pure, delicious love. The universe winked and waved every chance I gave it.

I remember sitting in a restaurant with our group of about 15. There was a swirl of activity amidst the din of patrons' chatter. Forks and spoons were clinking, waiters moved about taking orders and reciting specials. Amidst the cacophony, I sat in an oceanic stillness, enraptured by the glass of water before me. It was a gift I had not asked for, and it undid me. I could barely raise the glass to my mouth. It was as though all the secrets of creation were revealed in that solitary cup.

Maybe this sounds crazy.

Some people thought so, and I was hospitalized, diagnosed mentally ill, and prescribed a lot of medications. It was a confusing time because I thought I'd awoken at last, only to discover I'd been thrust deeply inside a nightmare. But angels illuminate the dark, and it was there that I found a path home to my true self.

It has taken years to walk this path, but what was once a desperate crawl has evolved into a climb back up the mountain of my true experience. My beloved corgi, Sydney, waddled patiently and exuberantly by my side through 12 years of growth, marriage, and children. He licked my tears in the dark and got me out of bed in the morning. His love was unconditional. Of all the pharmacies, psychiatrists, psychopharmacologists, no one was more "full of medicine" than my Sydney. He was an angel on this earth, and now though his body is no more, his gentle being infuses all

I do.

Although I didn't always, I now cherish my Israel experience. The very thing that seemed to elicit a complete "breakdown" actually planted the seeds of an inevitable "breakthrough". Powerful and creative though they may be, I believe our minds are not the foundation of our existence. I am not defined by thoughts.

I am capable of much more than I think, and when I connect with that deeper truth, I begin to experience the angel within. Her capacity to love and heal astounds me. She radiates a breathtaking peace and fearless love. And when I am able to put my life in her hands, I transcend my own limitations and experience life's deepest joys. I marvel at the mystery and revel in its truth: I am my own miracle. We all are.

Ashley, 50, Wilmington, DE

NAPTIME VISITOR

At six years of age, I was forced to take long naps every day. One afternoon asleep in the upstairs bedroom, I awoke to see a man I had never seen before sitting by an open window on my grandmother's upholstered Louis XVI *fauteuil*. Dressed in a buckskin fringed coat and wearing a coonskin hat, he was quietly staring at me; at times he would move slightly, crossing his legs or shifting the position of his hands, but he never spoke. Now this was not a dream, not a nightmare, and it happened in broad daylight.

Even though he seemed relaxed and not at all threatening, I was absolutely terrified. I couldn't move. For over an hour until my nurse came to awaken me, I lay there, and we simply looked at each other. During this time I came to understand that I could never tell anyone, even my beloved nurse, about what had happened because they would think I was crazy.

While not understanding at the time who he was or why he was there, I knew with total certainty that he *was* there, that this incident actually *did* happen. I never forgot this man; he changed my life. Seven years later on a European tour with my older sister, we visited Pompeii for the first time. Easily finding my way through the streets and alleys, I had a feeling that I had come home. Suddenly I knew I had had a past life there, a thought I never would have entertained had it not been for my naptime visitor.

Often the older we get, the more encumbered we are by layers of experience that deaden us emotionally, insulating us from the spiritual side of life. I've come to realize that my childhood visitor came to open me up to possibilities that I never would have considered before. Because of him I believe in angels, reincarnation, and life after death. He's helped me shed those outside layers, gifting me with a deeper understanding of the life of the soul.

John, 67, Palm Springs, CA

ANGELS WATCHING OVER US

Last year my husband and I decided to sell the house we had lived in almost forty years on Divisadero Street in San Francisco. A difficult decision, made more so because our sons were upset, we nonetheless declared it was time to move. They were grown, the house was too big for just the two of us and Meg, our black lab, and it had deferred maintenance, too much for our budget to handle.

We rushed it on the market, left for our camp in Montana, and then anxiously waited---and waited. Despite aggressive marketing and my many prayers, we didn't get one decent bid in six months. Two agents then recommended our moving out and investing a huge sum of money to remodel and stage our home. Adamant that we do neither, my husband dug in his heels in an "I-told-you-we-shouldn't-have-put-it-on-the-market-in-the-first-place" sort of way. There we were, in a stalemate, realizing we couldn't put our house back on the market as is and go through six more months of agonizing inactivity, and we couldn't afford to remodel and stage it at the price the agents mentioned. Frustrated and unhappy, we took it off the market.

A few days later we were at a Christmas party. An attractive, young couple, Barbara and Colin (whom we had *never* seen before, though we'd been neighbors for over a year) approached us and said, "We've been through your house and love it, but it needs a lot of work. We're exhausted from redoing our home. But we can give you some suggestions on what to do to sell yours and you can use our crew. They happen to need work right now, and we'll oversee the entire project for you."

I couldn't believe what I was hearing. Here were two people—complete strangers—sharing their insights on what we could do to sell our home and also offering us their workers. It was as if—without our saying anything—they understood our dilemma and wanted to help in any way they could. At exactly the right moment, two angels had shown up in our life.

My husband was suspicious; I felt his skepticism as he said, "We have a budget and I will not move out while the construction is going on!"

"No worries," replied Colin. "We can do the work with you there. It should take about 12 days, and I'm certain we can stay within your budget." Taking a deep breath, I said, "Yes, we'd love your help. We're ready to begin whenever you are." Despite my husband's finger poking my side, I added, "Thank you, thank you!"

The following week Colin's crew began work; true to his word they finished in 12 days, close to budget. Contacting our real estate agent, we told her we were ready to put our house back on the market. Thrilled after seeing the improvements, she arranged for a broker's open house. Before that ever happened, she called with wonderful news: We had a great offer—which we accepted. We had no hitches in closing, and within days we'd found a perfect house to rent.

After so many months of my praying to sell our home with no results, I had begun to think the angels weren't listening. Actually, they had been paying attention all along; they just knew better than I when the time was right for us to sell. Looking back I realized we hadn't been emotionally ready, at first, to let go of our home. If we hadn't met Colin or Barbara, we wouldn't be in our present house that we love so much. Humbled and forever grateful, I was reminded once again of the mystical workings of the Divine Plan. The angels were watching over us after all!

After the sale of our home, our 25 year-old son Nick stopped by Divisadero Street for the last time. We had a toast of champagne on the back porch and said goodbye to the place that had so many good memories.

"Mom, I just buried one of your stone angels in the backyard," Nick said. "I couldn't dig too deeply because I didn't have a shovel, but it is there to always watch over the house that helped make our family what it is today. I don't lament your decision to sell. But the memories are too meaningful for me to let this moment pass uncelebrated. One door closes, and another one opens. So here's to a new leaf, and here's to our being surrounded by angels. "

LB

A LAPSED CATHOLIC

Due to dire family circumstances, my father, at age five, boarded at a Catholic orphanage. Badly treated there, he carried painful memories that hastened his falling away from faith. After graduation from high school, he never entered a church, nor did he talk about his past. He did not want me, his daughter, baptized or raised in the church. When I was 25, my father died at the young age of 58, leaving me with more questions than answers about the role of religion in my life.

Ultimately, I became engaged to a wonderful man, a Catholic with two children, aged 11 and 13. A week before our marriage—on an Easter Sunday—he was away on a trip; I agreed to take his kids to St. Anselm's Catholic Church. As I was kneeling, I felt a liquid warmth wash over me, starting at the top of my head and enfolding my body.

I just knew my father was there blessing me, the children, and the path I was taking. Choosing the setting of this house of worship, he was validating my commitment to my new family and also letting me know he was happy, at peace, and no longer a lapsed Catholic.

Since being reunited with my father that Easter Sunday, I know there are angels everywhere who help us become more spiritual. After much consideration, three years ago after 24 years of marriage, I became a Catholic, and now my husband and I attend a small lovely church near our home. Recently, our twin grandchildren were christened there. Grateful to witness this continuation of faith through the next generation, I knew there were angels there surrounding all of us.

Kathy, 59, Ovando, MT

PORTRAIT OF AN ANGEL

After my son was born, I was eager to get pregnant again. But it was almost three years before we were blessed with a healthy beautiful baby girl. Then, at three months, she came down with what we thought was just a simple cold. After a visit to the doctor, she took a turn for the worse, and we rushed her to the hospital. Within the week she died from spinal meningitis.

Devastated, I couldn't stop crying, but my husband bottled up his emotions and refused to grieve. We never talked about the baby.

Instead we moved to the suburbs and concentrated on raising our son, a bright, good-looking boy.

Twenty years later, on vacation in Mexico, we received the terrible news that our son, now 23, had committed suicide. The day of his funeral, I remember looking at a painting my husband had bought at a local art show. It was a portrait of a woman standing beneath a bright blue sky. As I stood there, suddenly I saw wings sprouting out of both of her shoulders.

I kept looking at the painting, thinking, "What am I seeing? Am I hallucinating from all this stress and grief?" Calling my husband over, I said, "Do you remember her having wings?"

"No," he replied, stunned. For the first time since our baby daughter died, we cried together. Touched by the transformation of the painting, and the light now shining from it, we held each other tightly and felt comforted.

This experience opened me up to the idea there has to be much more to this life than we can ever imagine.

After the funeral, I could barely put one foot in front of the other. Soon I began having dreams, wonderful dreams I did not want to end. In all of them our son is there. He takes my hand and shows me his toys in his toy box, his socks neatly folded in a drawer, pages of his homework or pictures from his yearbook, or a scene of all of us sitting down together at the dinner table. Together, we are reviewing all the chapters of his life. "Thank you for the life you gave me," he says in one dream.

I feel this was his way of reassuring me he loved me, and telling me he is happy now. Thanks to those dreams, I began to understand I had a choice: I could feel sorry for myself, or I could enjoy the gift of life and help others come to terms with their painful losses.

These visitations from my son encouraged me to become involved with hospice and palliative care, and to support a camp for children who'd lost a parent or a sibling. I wanted create a safe place where people talk about their experiences of loss and openly grieve.

The deaths of my two children have given me a deeper sense of compassion and understanding. Even though these experiences have been unimaginably painful, I can now take a deep breath and feel grateful for the opportunities to grow in spiritual consciousness. I believe we all have guardian angels who walk among us and help us graduate into the light.

Gloria, 64, Winnetka, ILL.

NO COINCIDENCES

I believe that everything happens for a reason. There are no coincidences in our lives.

In 1938, before I was born, my aunt and a friend were driving along a country road near Glenbrook, Nevada. At sunset, the light was at such an angle making it difficult to see. They hit a cow as they were driving to a cocktail party. My aunt was thrown through the windshield and decapitated.

Seventeen years later, I went to boarding school in Massachusetts where I met my friend Ricky. He invited me to his grandmother's for

Thanksgiving. Realizing who I was, his grandmother said, "John, I was the other person in the car with your aunt the evening she died." Shocked by this wild coincidence, I wondered about the odds of our meeting. Ricky's family welcomed me into theirs, easing my homesickness and filling my years at boarding school with much laughter and fun. And somehow the cloud that had hovered over me because of my aunt's tragic death lifted.

This chance meeting changed my entire perspective and opened me up to spiritual possibilities I hadn't considered before. I realized there was something much bigger out there that I had ever imagined that erased any belief I'd had in coincidences. Right then I understood there is a God and a divine plan for all of us.

John, 72, San Francisco, CA

GUARDIAN ANGELS

Whether they were images in books my mother would read to me or words in songs I would sing at church or dreams I would have, angels were always present in my life. I was aware of spirits as well. As a young girl, I encountered a ghost, quite a mischievous one, who made a fork fly off our kitchen counter; another time he made a big bag of cat food slide across a shelf and drop to the floor. When my family and friends witnessed these strange happenings, too, they stopped thinking I was imagining him.

At one of my slumber parties my friends and I were standing in a dark hallway, with only a couple of candles to guide us—the electricity was out because of a storm. As a joke, I started talking to a picture of my brother, Tommy. Suddenly it started swinging back and forth. My friends dropped their candles and ran screaming from the house. This ghost was constantly reminding me that he was there and eager to play tricks whenever he could! Yet I've had positive experiences with angels as well.

There have been times when people have assumed the role of a guardian angel and come out of nowhere to help me, once even saving my life. As a 13 year-old growing up in Southern California, I spent a lot of time swimming in the ocean. Familiar and at ease with the currents and tides, I would bodysurf big waves and look at the ocean as my playground.

One day my older sister and I were bodysurfing and we got caught in a huge riptide. We literally could not move our legs when the tide pulled out. It was so strong it would suck water out to below our knees, and then the waves would crash over us, knocking us down and holding us under for a long time. We couldn't breathe or recover before the next wave hit us. We couldn't get to shore. At one point my sister got spit out. Even though I was screaming for help, she was in such a state of shock and exhaustion that she just walked slowly up the dunes towards where my mother lay, unaware of any danger.

Repeatedly pummeled and by then exhausted, I didn't want to go with the riptide; it was so huge, I knew I would be taken far out and be too tired to swim back to shore. There was no way I wanted to get swept out into the ocean where I would be totally alone. I remember thinking, "This is it, I'm too tired, I can't keep doing this. I'm going to die."

As I relaxed and let go, pictures of my life flashed before my eyes. In transition mode, I hadn't left my body but I felt peaceful, in a state of acceptance. The next thing I knew—a giant of a man appeared from nowhere, threw me over his shoulder and carried me out of the waves to my mother. He never said a word, just walked off.

Later, another giant came to my rescue. I was in the middle of my divorce and moving to a new house. Two friends were helping me transport a large Chinese armoire. At the end of the day, as I was backing my car down a long steep driveway below the Dipsea Steps in Mill Valley, I dropped into a gully that was steep and muddy. The more I tried to maneuver my car out of the ditch, the more it slipped; I was stuck. At the end of my rope, I burst out, "Oh my God, I can't do this! Father, Mother of God, I need a giant angel *right now* to come and help me move this car out of his ditch. Please, please send him to me." My friends thought I had gone crazy, but I was clear in my intention and was asking specifically for what I needed.

Suddenly in the rear view mirror I saw a giant of a man, easily 6'7" or 6'8" tall, running up the hill. He looked like Jaws in the James Bond movies, *Moonraker*. He was very muscular and I recognized him right away as the answer to my request. I dashed out of my car and asked him for help. I am not exaggerating when I say he effortlessly lifted up the back end of my car (against the gravity of the steep hill) and hoisted it out of the ditch while my friend put the car in drive.

Janine, 40, Mill Valley, CA

AN ANGEL FOR OTHERS

Just as human angels have helped me, I, too, have been graced with opportunities to save others. I was on the north shore of Kauai at Ke'e Beach, where there is a cove of still, very shallow water surrounded by a reef. People could walk out a great distance, and from afar it seemed as if they were walking on water. Carrying my 18 month-old son, I was walking in this lovely cove. A young boy I'd never seen before started following me. Enjoying the beauty of the shallow water and the surrounding land, I gave him little thought.

Suddenly the bottom dropped off steeply, and I found myself treading water and holding my son. The boy fell off the ledge as well, but he couldn't swim and was splashing wildly in the water. I kept trying to get him on his back, so I could swim him back to shallow water, but he was struggling against me, panicking and sinking. Yelling for help, I felt there was a moment I would have to let go of the boy to save my son, as I was struggling myself to maintain all three of us above water.

Fortunately someone came to our aid before I had to make this choice, and I was able to get all of us to shallow water. Shocked by how close this boy had come to drowning, I picked him up with one arm and carrying my son in the other, I marched 200 yards back to his parents, who had no idea he'd wandered off. I told them their son had almost drowned. Just as the giant in Southern California had saved my life, I had done the same for this child.

Another time, with help from my angel guides I saved my best friend from terrible tragedy. She was about to have her second child—a second home birth with the assistance of a doula. Even though her first birth was difficult, she was determined once again to avoid going to a hospital. To help out, I offered to take her two-year-old son during her birth process. After my friend and I had said our goodbyes, and her son and I were leaving, out of nowhere I got this very sad feeling along with the image of a dog whose puppy had just died. I knew I was receiving important information from my angel guides.

I turned to my dear friend and said, "You are going to get to a point in your labor where you'll feel something is wrong, very wrong, and your doula will doubt you, and say, 'No, keep pushing through this.' *Do not listen to her.* Get to the hospital immediately." This is exactly what happened.

Fortunately my friend remembered my words and was able to act on them, even in the height of her labor. She insisted that she be taken to the hospital. By the time she arrived, all her vital signs and the baby's were in the danger zone. She had an emergency C-section, and the doctors pulled out her baby daughter—blue and unresponsive—just in time to save the child.

The other day I went to the Apple Store. The lady working across from me kept looking over and smiling at me. We finally introduced ourselves, and I learned she was a minister at a church in San Anselmo. I asked if she ever gave sermons on angels. Pausing, she said "No, but now that you mention this, I think it's a wonderful idea." I left the store feeling happy that even the simple mention of angels can have a meaningful effect on others.

Janine, 40, Mill Valley, CA

AN ACCIDENT?

I remember the exact moment I realized I could no longer live the life I had been leading. I had graduated from college and was living on my own in Colorado. I had no direction. I was earning my way as a waitress at night and skiing during the day, not exactly a path to a promising career. And I was involved with an emotionally stingy guy who was verbally abusive. He constantly put me down, making me feel increasingly insecure. Though he was rarely kind or loving, I couldn't extricate myself from the relationship.

One day on the bus I saw some guys I didn't know that well who invited me to ski with them. The ski slope was one place where I felt confident and good about myself. Skiing with these friends all day, I felt happy and cherished. "Wow," I thought. "Life is wonderful." On the last run, Ed and I were racing. Catching an edge of my ski, I took a tremendous fall and heard my knee pop.

In that moment I knew the life I had been living was over. I couldn't waitress with this injury, and I knew my boyfriend wouldn't be at all supportive when he heard about the accident. As I was lying there on the ski slope, terrified and feeling completely alone, I suddenly felt protective arms wrap themselves around me, and I had a strong feeling I would be just fine. After I was carried off the mountain, I gathered my courage and called my parents and they welcomed me home—despite the fact that I had no job prospects and hadn't applied for the health insurance they were urging me to get.

After I recovered from my accident, I moved to a new city where I started from scratch. I found a teaching job that was challenging and fulfilling, and then met my future husband who loves me kindly and well. I am now creating a life full of promise. I look back to that hopeless moment on the ski slope and thank God and my angels for their reassuring messages of love and for guiding me through this difficult time.

Kris, 44, Belvedere, CA

HEALING ANGELS

I am a licensed acupuncturist, massage therapist, and herbalist. Before any healing session I ask for higher guidance from a group of guardian angels. Depending on the situation I will call on a specific angel. For example, when working with people in the middle of a divorce, I call upon the angels of communication who bring clarity and open-mindedness to the people involved. If I am trying to help someone release emotional traumas, I call upon the angels of transformation, transmutation, and integration who facilitate this change.

Years ago I bought a condominium in Hawaii that I later found out was built right next to a "Heiau," a place of worship in ancient Hawaii. Traditionally, human and animal sacrifices were made there. (This was one of several burial sites located throughout the complex.) I thought it was creepy and also a bit disrespectful to the dead. When I moved in, although the condo was new, there were many electrical problems; suddenly nothing would work, or the television would often turn on by itself.

I felt the spirits' presence, but refused to acknowledge them—which made them more persistent. A Hawaiian healer and friend explained to me that the old spirits wanted me to acknowledge and honor their presence. They were angry that white people had taken over their land, and they wanted recognition for what once was theirs.

A few years later I participated in a plan to create a healing center in Hawaii. The beauty of the valley of the proposed site, the ocean, palm trees, the light on the mountains swept me away, and I did not stop to consider and honor the history of this island and valley. Reserved for Hawaiian kings and the God Lono, the valley was the place of many battles and human sacrifices. Though I loved this valley, I couldn't sleep there. The few times I tried, spirits hovered over my face until I awoke. I was always startled. Luckily, I had two teachers, an energetic architect and a douser, who helped me rebuild the energetic structure of this land, creating more peace and harmony there. I learned to acknowledge and respect the spirits of this land, and my teachers and I ended up doing healings for 248 people who had died here.

The gifts I received were many healing flower essences made from local plants and the continual help from three land spirits—a teacher, a healer and a guide. One of their biggest messages to me was that I was to begin working in a co-creative way with the unseen helpers and guides.

Over the years, I have done healings for many who have died—especially when their deaths were by suicide. Perhaps because I understand that the veil between the seen and unseen is very thin and perhaps because I am very sensitive to the beings on the other side, they seem to find me. I work with what we call discarnates, those who are out of their bodies but whose spirits have not yet moved on. They see death as final, and this lack of understanding inhibits them from moving on to another plane.

In these scenarios, I ask the angels of healing and communication to assist them and explain that they're just out of body. I also call in the angels of transition to help them understand they are just changing form and moving to another plane, that nothing is final, that they are truly infinite beings of light.

Janet, 46, Corte Madera, CA

ANSWERS TO MY PRAYERS

Whenever I have personal trouble, I pour my heart into a prayer. Afterwards, I will be listening to the radio, and a song or a discussion will come on that speaks to my precise difficulty.

Recently, I downloaded the entire Bible on an MP3. If you listened to it 24/7 nonstop, it would take you over a week to get through the whole volume. At the time I was having family problems and decided to turn on my MP3, which has a random feature, and listen to whatever passage from the Bible came on. The first sentence of the passage that played was as if someone were speaking directly and specifically to me to address my problem.

The chances of this happening are so rare—there *has* to be something or someone out there that's much larger than we could ever imagine. Experiences like this reinforce my belief in God and the angels who I know are guiding us and giving us the answers to our prayers.

Anthony, 30, San Rafael, CA

SAN SEBASTIAN

Eleanor Roosevelt said, "You must do the thing you cannot do," while Elizabeth Taylor told an interviewer, "I've never regretted the things I did—only the things I didn't do." As I neared my 59th birthday, I was trying to follow this advice, but at times it was difficult.

Our youngest son Nick, 20 at the time, a junior at Boston College, had decided to take his second semester abroad to study in San Sebastian, Spain. Since he would be turning 21 there, I was toying with the idea of visiting him. "Fine," my husband said. "But count me

out. It's too far to travel for anyone's birthday."
My anxiety about traveling alone outweighed
my eagerness to see my son, and I quickly
forgot about any advice to challenge myself.

One day Nick called. "Mom, my 21st birthday
is coming up. Why don't you come for a visit
then?"

"Nick, you don't really want your old Mom
coming to visit on your big birthday, do you?
I'd cramp your style."

"Seriously, Mom, I want you to come. You can
meet my friends and see how wonderful San
Sebastian is."

Crossing my fingers, I took a long breath, and
said, "Yes, yes, I'd love to come. What a great
idea!"

The good news was that I was able to get a free
mileage ticket; the bad news was that I had
many connections to make before reaching my

destination. As my departure neared, I felt increasingly anxious, consumed with the fear of losing my way, so I armed myself with some Ambien. When my husband dropped me off at the airport, my stomach was churning. I checked my purse obsessively, touching my passport, credit cards, ticket and money. I am embarrassed to admit that this ritual continued throughout the entire trip.

Boarding in San Francisco, I sat next to an interesting teacher and mother of three. We were soon sharing stories about our children, and by the time we landed in New York, I felt more relaxed. On the next leg of my trip, my seatmate was an attractive young Spanish woman who taught school in Palo Alto. Energetic and kind, she was on her way home to visit her sick mother. When we arrived in the immense Madrid airport, she took charge, going well out of her way to lead me from Terminal 1 to Terminal 3. It was then I realized I was in the hands of angels.

Waiting for my next flight that didn't appear on any monitor, I was approached by a lovely Spanish woman who addressed me in her native tongue. I shook my head. She then spoke a bit of English, explaining she was flying to San Sebastian and concerned about the lack of information on the flight. I was frantic. After heated conversations with agents, she told me to stay by her side. Finally, we were bussed to a small plane, far away from the gates.

For the next hour and a half, we flew through dense clouds—visibility almost zero. Touching my tiny angel pin I kept in my purse, I closed my eyes. As we made our final, bumpy approach, from my rain-streaked window, I could see the huge, choppy waves of the Atlantic Ocean. My heart was pumping, and I began to sweat, but the plane landed without incident. Carolina, my new angel, gave explicit directions to my cab driver, and soon I arrived at my hotel. Opening my door, I was thrilled to see sweet Nick leaning in to give me a hug.

The sun came out, and we had six wonderful days together. We enjoyed an amazing dinner at Arzak, traveled to Biarritz for the weekend, read together on the beach, shopped, and drank champagne. Here in Spain, I saw a new Nick, a young man taking charge of his life. I was happy he could share this rite of passage and reassured to see he was finding his way in a foreign country.

We celebrated his 21st birthday with fourteen of his friends at a Basque restaurant. Dressed in a brown leather jacket and a striped Spanish shirt, Nick was a commanding presence. As I raised my glass to toast him, I saw how much I would have missed had I not taken up this challenge.

Carrying home amazing memories of my trip, I was forever grateful that I had decided to go. I quietly thanked all those angels who had taken my hand and guided me. Not only did they help me find my way, they lifted me up so I could have a clearer view of what is important in this life on earth.

P.S. When I got home, Nick called to say. "Happy Mother's Day to the best mother in the world." I asked him for an update on his life. "Perfecto, Mom," he said. "Perfecto."

LB

ANGEL ON MY SHOULDER

One afternoon I was zooming down Bush Street, a fast commuter artery into downtown San Francisco. Intent on my driving, I remember feeling relieved the lights were in synch. I was pressing the speed limit, when I felt a tap on my shoulder, causing me to look to my left. There I saw a tiny Chinese girl (she couldn't have been more than 18 months old) toddling, all by herself, down the sidewalk of this very busy street.

Instinctively, I pulled over, jumped out of my car and picked up this child. There was no one else on the block. As I wandered down the street wondering what to do, I noticed an open door of an old Victorian house. When I rang and rang the bell, finally a very sleepy Chinese grandmother appeared. Glaring at me, she grabbed the child, said something I didn't understand, and closed the door. Obviously, it had been naptime, but the grandmother had been the only one asleep!

I would have driven by this child in two seconds and never seen her, but something very powerful got my attention. I've never forgotten this incident; I can't explain it, and have often wondered about it. I am grateful I was in a position to help this child; perhaps she had guardian angels watching over her. I'd like to think maybe I was one of them. This experience made me consider the possibility that there is something beyond that guides and protects us.

Helen, 55, San Francisco, CA

HOPE AND LOVE

Born to an upper class Serbian family with banking interests, I led a charmed life in Belgrade until the start of WWII. When I was five, our entire family was celebrating Easter at my grandparents' estate in Belgrade. Sharing a bedroom with several of my cousins, I was awakened by a frightening noise. Suddenly the entire house was shaking, there was dust everywhere, and when I looked over at the other beds where my cousins were supposed to be sleeping, they were empty.

Grabbing my teddy bear, I wandered through the house, but no one was there. When hours before, our house had been filled with the laughter of my parents, grandparents, aunts, uncles and cousins, now it was silent. Terrified, I ran back to my bed, pulled the covers over my head. As I lay there, shaking and tightly holding onto my bear, I heard him say, "Don't worry, be calm, I am with you. Everything will be OK." Immediately, I calmed down and was comforted. And then my aunt appeared, picked me up, and rushed me down to the cellar. I had been overlooked in the panic of Hitler's bombing, his retaliation against Serbia for not joining the war pact with Germany, Italy, and Japan.

I wasn't aware then that this lonely nighttime conversation was my first experience with angels. But during those years of war and then communist oppression, I would talk to my teddy bear and be consoled. Obviously, the toy did not speak but was the conduit, enabling me to focus on my angels and call upon them.

A career army general staff officer, my father was captured by the Germans and sent to a POW camp in 1941. In April 1943 when I was six, my mother, sister and I were once again visiting my grandmother when bombs, this time dropped by British and American allies, were devastating Belgrade, now occupied by Nazi Germans. Deciding to leave for the country, my grandmother had ordered a car but we had to walk 50 blocks through rubble and torn-up streets to get to it. Off we went, my grandmother holding tightly to my hand, and my mother carrying my two year-old sister.

Suddenly sirens went off again, a warning that bombing was imminent. We had to get inside to stay alive. On our immediate right was a sturdy six-story building where a school friend of my mother's lived. My mother and grandmother turned towards the entrance, but I stopped in the middle of the street and refused to go. It was as if I were frozen in place on the sidewalk, as if some invisible hand were holding me back and pushing me hard in the other direction. Though they were yelling and screaming at me, I managed to pull away from my grandmother and run across the street towards a two-story house. They had to follow me. Somehow we got to the basement as the bombing commenced.

The bombs fell everywhere. The house shook as if as if in the throes of a violent earthquake. Water pipes burst, and at one point hidden in the house's cellar, we thought we were hit. Yet, I felt calm and observed the panic and devastation with a childlike bewilderment. When the raid was over, we looked across the street to the building where my mother and grandmother had wanted to go. It had taken a direct hit, and all that was left was a big, gaping hole.

In October 1944 when I was 8, the Communists took over Yugoslavia. Although they allowed our family to stay in my grandfather's house, they took everything of value, and leaving us to starve. Because of our family's capitalist background, they shot several male members of our family, including my beloved uncle who had given me the teddy bear. Economic and other living conditions were terrible; everything was rationed. We survived because my grandfather, the banker, had hidden gold coins, which we would use to buy food and clothes on the black market. A few years later, my mother was jailed, and the government threatened to take custody of my six-year-old sister and me.

At age 16, I realized I had to leave Belgrade, for there was no future for me under the Red Star of Communism. However, the borders were sealed by the Iron Curtain. Somehow, my uncle in Paris found a peasant farmer in

Slovenia, whose land lay partly across the border into Italy, who was willing to smuggle me across. Of course this was very dangerous because the Communists were shooting many people who tried to escape. I was set to go in the spring of 1955 but received a message I would have to wait until the next year. I did not know why.

Unexpectedly, a new door opened in December. I had just finished one year of law at Belgrade University when, by bribing an official, one of my grandfather's lawyers secured a passport for me to attend the Sorbonne in Paris to do some legal research. I went before a commissar at the Ministry of the Interior, saying I had to leave that very night. He handed me a passport.

At the time I was in love with a wonderful young woman. We were thinking of getting married once I had finished my university education. I told no one, including her, anything about my departure, so there would be no accomplices, no one who could be blamed and punished by cruel communists. I packed one suitcase with basic essentials (and of course my teddy bear) and got on the train that would ultimately take me to freedom. I have never known if the passport was a forgery.

There were many guards at the border checking passports. I was hardly able to control my fear. My hands were trembling, my knees shaking. But once again it was as if I heard my teddy bear's voice: "Be calm, be cool, all will be fine, and you will get where you are going." I settled down, and the passport inspection went off without a hitch. I got the train to Venice and then transferred to the Venice-Paris Overnight Express.

In Paris, I was supposed by law to receive an entrance visa to America immediately, as my father was an American citizen. Yet I met with unexpected delays for the next nine months. Much later, I realized my guardian angels were deciding when I would arrive in the US, start university and meet my future wife. Had I not left Belgrade in December 1955 and instead decided to wait until the following spring, I would not have met my wife. I may never have gotten out of Yugoslavia, or worse, I might have been shot at the border crossing.

I didn't understand until many years later there have been guardian angels watching over me since my birth—even causing what felt like interference and frustration. They have actually been guiding me through crucial times, starting with that desperate moment in April 1941 when I was alone and petrified by the bombing, and comforted by my teddy bear.

Michael, 74, San Rafael, CA

MY BELOVED BROTHERS

I get in touch with my angels and converse with them; fundamental principles govern our interactions. The most important one is that I can, at every crossroad of my life, make my own decision as to what to do, since our Creator endowed us with free will. However, there have been many moments when flying the airplane of my life, someone, an invisible pilot, has grabbed the wheel and steered me elsewhere.

One such moment was late one night when I was driving my sister and her friend back to Monterey. We were going 60 miles an hour on a dark, two-lane road. At a curve I saw a car coming straight at us the wrong way. My natural instinct was to move into the other lane to avoid the oncoming car, but I could not turn the steering wheel. The other car came so close its lights were blinding; then it swerved into the other lane. Had I followed my impulse, we would have run off the road, flipped and been seriously injured.

I began reading books on comparative religions and was particularly interested in the American psychic Edgar Cayce. Introduced to the most illuminated spirit I had ever met on earth, a minister of a small church in San Francisco, I spent seven years studying metaphysics and other spiritual matters with her. This is when I established direct contact with my angels.

Our family bought a small house in the Sierras where I would go to read, meditate and be away from people and urban energies. One time I was meditating and someone—in a soundless voice—started 'talking' to me. "There are three of us who are spiritual brothers of yours. We have been with you from your birth."

"How do I get in touch with you?" I asked. "When you're quiet, envision three symbols--a pillow with a simple gold crown on top, another holding an old-fashioned silver key, and the last, a big hammer. These three symbols represent the spiritual, mental and physical parts of your life." Meditating on them brought me a deep sense of comfort.

These beloved brothers made it clear they would never support me in gaining material wealth and power for myself. And they would never interfere with my free will, the ultimate gift from God. The essence of love, they told me, is the gift of freedom to be your self.

Several times these angels have brought me messages from departed loved ones, my uncle who gave me the teddy bear for one. The Angels of Karma helped my father and me understand that our relationship in a past life had negatively impacted us in this one. With their aid, we reconciled.

Finally, my angel guardians and brothers in God, the Creator of all known and unknown, have helped me in my never-ending search to understand the mysteries of life. These angels have illuminated the pathways of my soul. They have led me to accept that life is eternal and boundless, and that love waits at the end. For this incomparable gift, I am forever grateful.

Michael, 74, San Rafael, CA

OLIVIA

U nless you've lost a child, you could never walk in my shoes. When at 12, after a three-year struggle with cancer, Olivia, my only daughter, died, I would have succumbed to total despair, had it not been for her and the courageous, selfless example she set. Though she knew she was dying, she never once felt sorry for herself. Instead she focused her heart on me, knowing that I would soon be alone without the person I loved most in life.

"Don't do anything crazy after I'm gone," she said. Olivia made me promise to survive, to carry on and live fully for her sake, and she told me she would always be watching over me. The instant she passed, I felt her presence leave the room and go out the window. It was a beautiful day, and I couldn't stop weeping. At the moment I couldn't bear to be alive now that my daughter was no longer on this earth. Then I felt her nearby and was reminded of my promise.

A week after Olivia's death, I decided to drive across the country and leave my car with my parents, who were living on the east coast. My first stop along the way was Santa Fe. Walking into one of the many art galleries there, I was struck dumb by an exquisite statue of two women, the one in front with angel wings. The title of this three-foot sculpture was "Guardian Angel." I thought it was incredibly beautiful but couldn't afford it.

I continued on my road trip, stopping in Oklahoma City to visit a close friend. I couldn't stop talking about this sculpture that spoke to me so strongly. It evoked Olivia's spirit, reminding me that my daughter was now my guardian angel. My girlfriend understood and convinced me to sell my car and use the proceeds buy the sculpture.

A year later to the day of Olivia's death, I entered a bike race to raise money for leukemia research. Though I had not been on a bike for years, was out of shape and mentally unprepared, I rode in this 100 mile event in Santa Fe, a place of great spiritual solace for me. During the race, I felt Olivia egging me on.

The pain of her passing is always there, but with time it feels less raw. Knowing she is nearby guiding and inspiring me helps me to continue to live life to the best of my ability.

Laura, 45, Denver, CO

MY GABBY GIRLS

Yes, I most certainly believe in angels. I have two, in particular, who are always nearby—my mother and Ginny, my best friend. In life, both were outgoing and energetic. You couldn't miss them in a room full of people. Accomplished and confident, they met life head-on, eager to handle whatever challenging situations life might present to them. They were big talkers. I called them my gabby girls. They were never afraid to take a stand, whether by word or by action, for what they felt was right, while I was quiet and not very brave about speaking up.

When Ginny was dying, I flew east and spent 10 days by her side, holding her hand and trying to comfort her as best I could. We shared stories of our long friendship. We laughed, and we cried. Then because of family demands I reluctantly had to leave her side, but not before she promised she would always watch over me. The day after I got home, I took a walk. It was a cold, grey day. In the distance I noticed a woman with long blond hair, dressed in a turquoise blue jogging suit, walking towards me. She had a golden retriever on a leash. Ginny *also* had long blond hair, a blue warm-up suit, and a golden retriever.

As we passed each other, this stranger looked at me and smiled a joyous smile. At that very moment the sun broke through the grey clouds. When I got home from my walk, the phone rang; it was Ginny's daughter calling to tell me what I already had intuited — that her mother had just died, peacefully, with her family around her. And because of my recent encounter, I knew that Ginny was radiantly happy where she was and felt that she and my mother, who had died recently, were now together, cheering me on.

No longer afraid to speak up, I thank both my beloved mother and dear friend, my gabby girls, for the courageous examples they set. I feel them by my side, still comforting and guiding me, whispering words of encouragement, especially in situations where I need to be courageous. Grateful for their continued presence in my life, I take heart.

Mary, 70, Cape Cod, MA

45 SECONDS

Trained as a scientist, I tend to approach life with a rational point of view. However, I have had some experiences that I cannot explain with logic. Once in the middle of the night, I was awakened from a deep sleep by the sound of my close friend's voice calling my name. Though he lived 20 miles away I heard it clear as a bell. In the morning I found out that he had died at exactly the time I heard his voice.

When my mother-in-law was in the hospital, my wife stayed by her side, while I went home with our children. At 2:45 A.M. I awoke to hear my mother-in-law calling my name and saw her shadow running past me. I assumed she had died and this was her way of saying goodbye. When my wife came home much later, she told me her mother had passed and I said, "Yes, I know... at 2:45 this morning."

One vacation my wife and I were staying at a bed and breakfast inn in Northern California. Again, something woke me up, and when I looked at the foot of the bed, I saw a couple standing there in wedding garb. I poked my wife, and she saw them as well. We then closed our eyes, hoping they would disappear. The next morning we told the owner what we saw and asked, "Are we hallucinating?"

"No," he explained. "Other guests have seen these ghosts. A couple came here for their honeymoon and stayed in your room. After they left, they were killed in a car accident. I think they were returning to the last place where they were happy."

Another time I was driving to Lake Tahoe with a friend. We were on a small, scenic road, and ahead of us there was a commotion, and then a car flipped over. Arriving on the scene of the accident, we saw a young man standing off to the side, obviously in shock, and then I noticed a woman's arms and head hanging upside down out of the window. There was smoke and licks of flame coming from the car. I ran over, pulled her out and took her over to her companion.

This was all over in 45 seconds. I got back into our car, and we drove off. This incident seemed like a dream until we read about the accident in the paper and learned that both people had survived. Perhaps I was that woman's guardian angel just for 45 seconds. I did what I needed to do to save her life and then moved on.

Julio, 55, Larkspur, CA

SENT BY ANGELS

My husband and I had just returned from an amazing trip to Argentina. Still swept up in memories of our wonderful guides, of big brown trout, pristine rivers snow-capped mountains, we found it hard to reenter our lives in San Francisco. We missed sitting around blazing fires, and looking up at the star-studded sky—the Southern Cross in all its glory.

One Saturday, I was so homesick for Argentina I got dressed up and did something completely out of character. On a whim, I donned my gaucho pants, leather belt and espadrilles, and in this outfit I went downtown to shop—an activity I generally avoid. As I was walking down Stockton Street, an attractive, young couple approached me and asked, "Are you from Argentina?"

"No," I said. "But I have just returned from there. Are you?"

"Yes," they nodded, enthusiastically. We chatted for a few minutes, and on an impulse, I invited them for dinner.

When I returned home, my husband said, "You asked a couple *you just met on the street* for dinner?" I explained that they were so nice *and* they were from Argentina, *and* they were probably missing their family. "Besides," I said. "I just wanted to." A man of few words, he said, "Fine."

A few days later, Juan and his wife Vico came for dinner. We had a wonderful time, and despite our difference in ages, became good friends. Since we had few details of their backgrounds (their surname meant nothing to us), we just assumed they were the typical struggling young couple.

Six months later Juan mentioned that his parents were coming for a visit, and so we invited all of them for dinner. As soon as Juan, Sr. and his wife, Isabel, arrived, I felt an immediate connection. At the end of the evening they invited us to come to their ranch in Uruguay. A year later, after fishing in Patagonia, we stepped on the ferry that would take us across the Rio de la Plata to Uruguay. Not having a clue of what to expect, we were simply excited to see Juan Sr. and Isabel again, especially so because our young friends, would be there as well.

Arriving at their home we were welcomed by their entire family, Juan's parents, his two sisters, their husbands, and their children, with open arms and delightful smiles. Later we had a barbeque by the river and then a tour of their immense, beautiful property. One afternoon we walked the Stations of the Cross leading up to their private chapel. At every station, there was a painting of Christ's tortured journey to His crucifixion. Walking through this leafy arbor, feeling the soft grass beneath our feet, we felt as if we had been touched by angels. Later, we celebrated Juan's birthday in the chapel with wooden benches beneath exquisite stained glass windows, the children singing and playing their guitars.

During our entire visit, my husband and I felt constantly surrounded by unconditional love. We were deeply moved, our hearts touched by their grace. We returned to America but our lives were busy, as were theirs. One day recently when we gathered together at Stinson Beach, Juan delivered his unexpected news:

They had decided to move back permanently to Argentina. Now with four young children, they wanted to be close to their family and raise their children in the life they had known.

While happy for them, I was devastated that we might never see each other again.

Juan told me he felt it was God's will that we met so long ago. He said, "You have no idea how much you mean to us and how deeply we carry you in our hearts."

I recalled how I felt when Bill and I went to visit them: I closed my eyes, and imagined we were part of their beautiful family. I understand now that our encounter on the streets of San Francisco was not a random one, but rather destined to be. Shining their light on us, they made us feel beloved.

LB

KELSEY, OUR ANGEL

Kelsey, our beloved golden retriever, always thought she was a person. The light of our lives, she loved us all, my wife, our two children, and me. The kids had great fun throwing tennis balls for Kelsey that she would happily retrieve for hours on end, or lying on top of her when saying goodnight as she lay in her dog bed, or watching her chase leaves that spun through our backyard. When the kids were at school, however, she was my closest companion because I worked from home, and she never left my side.

When she got older and had trouble walking around the block, the vet diagnosed her with cancer and said she only had a few days to live. We brought her home for one last weekend of unconditional love. We spent the entire time petting her, feeding her favorite snacks of peanut butter and cookies, throwing her a tennis ball, telling her how much we loved her. At sunset we even took her for one last walk on the beach where we told her it was okay if she had to go. Late Sunday evening, she was laboring to breathe, and it was obvious her time had come. After getting the kids to bed, we had her put down around midnight.

The next morning, we were numb with grief. After dropping off our children at school, my wife and I drove to a field where I often play softball. We walked to the mound, and there on top was a tennis ball. In the many times I have either practiced or played softball there, I have never seen a tennis ball. Later that day, we grabbed sandwiches and headed to the beach. Right next to the table we randomly picked was another tennis ball. As we stared at it, a seven-month old Golden Retriever came running over to us and nuzzled between us.

At that moment we both realized that all day Kelsey had been trying to communicate with us, to assure us she was fine and she loved us. I picked up the ball and threw it hard and far, and the puppy took off like a rocket. Comforted, we laughed when the puppy paused, looked over at us, and then ran to its owner with the ball.

Robert, 50, Greenwich, CT

DAISY AND ROSIE

After Daisy, our beloved black and white Border Collie, died, my wife and I went away for two weeks. The very day of our return, I looked out into our garden, and there hiding under a rose bush staring at me was a black and white cat, sporting the exact same markings and coloring of our late collie. We made inquiries, discovering that the cat *belonged* to a family up the hill from us. The father was allergic to cats and his daughter, the owner, had been away in college, and so for years this cat was left to its own devices, sleeping in their garage and roaming the hills.

Since the owner was now back, she picked up her cat that was now 'residing' in our garden. Halfway home, the cat jumped out the window of the car and ran back to our garden. For years, ever since her owner had left, she'd obviously been watching us, and when Daisy died, she decided to come to us. Soon she started venturing through the doggie door, and finally ended up sleeping on our bed every night. We named her Rosie in honor of her hiding place.

I have never been a cat lover, we have never owned a cat, but my wife and I love Rosie. We have no explanation for the timing of Rosie's arrival in our lives other than Daisy sent her to us to console us. This was not a coincidence.

Steve, 47, Mendocino, CA

SHADOW

Rivers are woven into the story of my life; their light and shadows pierce my soul, drawing me to what lies below their surface beauty, to what I can't see but only imagine. This yearning to explore the depths plays out throughout my life. We all have rivers of our own, separate ones that carry us forward, but ones that begin and end together.

Growing up on our family's ranch in Northern California, I spent much time along two little rivers that graced our property. These waters of my youth wrapped themselves around my heart, and after we lost the ranch, I searched elsewhere to find a replacement. Now spending summers in Montana, my husband and I camp by the North Fork of the Blackfoot River. I hear its call and can't resist running to its side. I love its sparse, deep pools, eddies and rushing riffles, its clean mineral smell mixed with mint and pine.

Alone in camp one day with Shadow, our beloved black lab, I sat down to read *Little Rivers* by Margot Page. I came to the part when her mother is dying: Margot is sitting next to her, holding her hand in the darkness of her bedroom, when her stiff-upper-lip-Yankee mother says, in a voice choked with pain, "I'll miss helping you with your babies."

I cried, remembering how much I had yearned for my mother to witness and cherish me as a mother to my three sons. But she died two years before Christian, my first, was born.

As I wept, Shadow, my little black angel, an old dog full of aches and pains, awakened and put her head on my lap, then licked my hands and legs. For a long while she stayed close to me, her wise brown eyes searching mine. Many times Shadow has eased the loneliness in my heart and helped me remember the many gifts I have in my life.

LB

ANIMALS AND ANGELS

When I first started holding seminars for women in life transition, my Maine Coon Cat Zoe played a strong role in our weekly gatherings. Each time we met, Zoe recognized the member of the group who was feeling most vulnerable and settled in her lap. For several years, she continued to offer much-needed TLC to all of the participants. Was my cat seeing energy patterns, auras? How did she know what lap to go to every time?

Recent research shows that animals can see UV light, tuning into wavelengths so refined they're inaccessible to the human eye. Perhaps this is what allows them to sense changes in our mood and emotional field. There are also reports that animals are able to detect ghost or spirits.

The other day I was reminded of the Old Testament tale of Balaam's Donkey (*Numbers 22: 21-39*) that shows how exquisitely sensitive animals can be — and how genuinely concerned for our welfare. After 40 years of wandering, the Israelites were about to settle down. The King of Moab didn't want them in the neighborhood, so he sent a messenger to Balaam, a well-known seer, asking him to denounce the newcomers. Balaam agreed to meet with the king and discuss this strategy.

On the way, his donkey approached a turn in the road and halted. With the whip, Balaam urged him on. The donkey backed up, scraping Balaam's foot against a wall. Furious, Balaam used the whip again trying to force his mount back into the middle of the road, but the animal wouldn't budge.

In a moment of mercy, the Lord gave the animal the ability to speak. "What have I done to you to make you beat me three times?" the donkey asked.

"You have made a fool of me!" said Balaam.

"Am I not the faithful donkey you have always ridden? Am I in the habit of doing things like this?"

Balaam shook his head, knowing he was in the wrong. Then he looked up and saw an angel with a bright sword, standing in the road.

"I came here to stop you because what you are about to do is reckless," the angel said. "Your donkey saw me and turned away three times. If he had not stopped, I would have killed you. But on no account would I have harmed your animal."

Balaam knelt down before the angel and begged forgiveness. Then he rode on to his meeting to deliver a different message to the Moabites.

"I can't say whatever you please," he told the King, refusing to denounce the Israelites. "I must speak only the words that God puts in my mouth."

With their extra sensitivity, animals are attuned to the Holy Spirit. Working in concert with the angel, the donkey taught Balaam true humility and enabled him to do God's will.

Valerie, 66, Mill Valley, CA

NEVER-ENDING LOVE

Katie Ann Conway, our beloved daughter, moved on to the next life five days shy of her 15th birthday. My husband always said she was an old soul with knowledge beyond this earth. We were the proudest parents ever, but we take no credit. God gave us a remarkable gift in our daughter, and I believe He sent her here to teach us how to love.

A straight-A honor student, Katie loved everyone, especially her family and friends. The last picture I have of her was taken a few days before she died. She is with Emily, one of her best pals, who wished she were 5'9" like Katie. Katie positioned herself to make Emily appear taller then said, "Remember, it's not what you look like. It's what is in your heart."

Even though she suffered from severe asthma, Katie made the high school swim team, and this exercise was good for strengthening her lungs. We would wake at 5 A.M., pick up other girls who were groggy and still half asleep, and head for the local community college for practice. In the car, Katie played spirited, let's-get-going-and-win songs, and soon everyone was awake and singing. The coaches said her loving spirit and enthusiasm was integral to the team's success, and they later organized an annual fundraiser in her honor.

Two years before Katie died, I joined a real estate firm run by Mary Davis. I do not doubt for one second that God put Mary and me together for the beautiful reason that she would be there (and I mean *right there*, since we worked in the same office) to help me get though Katie's moving on. Mary's son, Kevin, had died years before in a car accident, and she had become a grief counselor for parents who lost their children. When I still had my Katie, I would watch these parents come to talk with Mary and wonder how they could get through the day after enduring such a terrible loss.

In 2004, Katie's doctor said her asthma was under control. On May 4 we went shopping for a confirmation dress and then out to dinner. When we got home, Katie went upstairs to hang up her new dress. Suddenly she reappeared and gasped, "Mom, I'm not breathing." I immediately plugged in the nebulizer. After a few seconds, she looked at me and said, "Not working." I called 911.

Mary, friend and boss, was also a volunteer ambulance driver. She *happened* to be on duty that night, heard my distress call, and showed up at our door. The EMTs rushed Katie to the hospital, but she died in the ambulance. She had gone into full respiratory arrest. Mary was there by my side to help me bear this tragedy.

That week Katie had come home from school and said, "Mom, do you know what my confirmation teacher told us today in class?" I shook my head. "That if we do our best, God will do the rest." She paused, adding, "It takes the pressure off, right Mom?"

As a mother you always want your children to be happy. Even when they're not with you any longer, you still hope for that. In many ways and through many people, Katie has communicated to us that she is very happy and for us not to worry. Once I dreamt that we were walking shoulder to shoulder. Katie was laughing and full of energy and light. Then she kept on walking.

Mary and I talk about our children every day. We both collect angels and have each had a similar dream about our children. They came to reassure us—but we couldn't touch them. They were behind a wall of glass. We knew they were in Heaven, and we could see them beaming and cheering us on.

My close friend Gail, who always had a strong connection to the other side, once dreamt of Katie in a lovely white dress, looking beautiful and happy. In her teens Katie struggled with eczema. In Gail's vision, she was radiant and had perfect skin.

Not long after Katie's death, my sister-in-law, Cathie, went to a teacher's annual get-together. Cathie had no idea that the hostess had invited a medium. Uncomfortable with the notion of life after death, my sister-in-law had shown no interest in the other side or in any of my spiritual beliefs. When the session commenced, the medium said, "There is a young girl here who has passed over. She's full of energy and wants to communicate. Does anyone know who she is?"

Cathie said nothing. No one else responded. At the end of the session, the medium said, "That young girl is still with us." Finally Cathie admitted that she had lost her niece. The medium passed on a message. "She wants her brother to know she was at his wedding and had a wonderful time. She is very happy about the name he gave his baby daughter — Ava Katie — and she is watching over her."

When Cathie told me this, I was thrilled. Through the medium Katie had said one more thing, "Please tell my father that I will always be his Daddy's Girl." I was floored. I'd just mentioned to my husband that our new granddaughter Ava Katie was going to be a real Daddy's Girl just like her namesake.

The year after my daughter's death, I had a closing on a big home, and the kitchen needed a good cleaning. Unable to sleep, I drove there at 6 A.M. and started to work. As I scrubbed drawer after drawer, I remember thinking, "Katie died and here I am taking care of someone else's mess. What is this about?" Teary-eyed, and feeling sorry for myself, I yanked open another drawer and out popped an angel statue with the words "I love you, Mom" written on the base. For Katie's last birthday, I had bought this same angel with "Happy Birthday" inscribed on it. In that moment, I knew beyond a doubt Katie was there, telling me she would never stop loving me, and that one day we would all be reunited.

Trudy, 53, Oradell, NJ

BEYOND WORDS

On the day I turned 33, my beloved father died. He was 85. That night, after I went to bed I felt his presence. He grasped my hand and held it for a long time. I knew this was his final goodbye, done in his typical quiet, loving way. I don't have the words to describe this encounter.

Years later, my father-in-law was dying in a veteran's hospital. After visiting him there, my husband came home and we went to bed. At 2 AM I was awakened by a noise at our bedroom window. Still half-asleep, I saw a black bird perched on the sill and realized that my father-in-law had died.

Things like this often happen that make me aware I am connected to something much larger than day-to-day worries. I will telephone my brother, a close friend or even someone I haven't seen in a long time, and invariably they will exclaim, "I was just thinking of you!" I realize these are just the tip of the iceberg in terms of communication between people; I am aware of how little I know and how much there is to learn about this reality in my heart that is beyond words. I believe there is a much higher purpose, a much higher consciousness that I'm not even aware of. I am in a constant state of awe.

Roberta, 50, Reno, NV

EXPANDING HORIZONS

I t took several experiences for me to learn to trust in the spiritual realm.

Some years ago my husband and I and our two daughters were getting ready for a trip to our vacation home at Tahoe. As was our habit, he and I would share the driving responsibilities. While packing I had a vision of myself driving in the mountains and the car being forced off a steep cliff. I went to my husband, and said "I can't help you with the driving." When we were high in the Sierras, I suddenly recognized the place I had seen in my vision and had chills from head to toe. But back then I didn't see this as an angel warning me. Now I believe that it was.

Twenty-five years ago a dear friend developed colon cancer that metastasized to her liver. Without any family during her last months, she relied heavily on another close friend and me. We cared for her personal business, saw her every day, and monitored all the hospitalization procedures. One day she was in a great deal of pain, and as I prepared to depart for work, she said, "Please don't leave." I told her I would return later that day, but when I did, she had lapsed into a coma. She passed away that night.

The next afternoon I took a walk. There was an open meadow next to me. As I looked toward the sky in the west, I saw a beautiful being come into my field of vision. I realized it was my friend. Peaceful, smiling, her smile incredibly beautiful, she said, "It's all wonderful. From now on, I'll be near you, watching over you." Once again at that time in my life, I didn't give a conscious thought or any credibility to the possibility of a spiritual being communicating with me.

Several years later I was in very difficult partnership with another woman. The challenges of my business on top of this destructive relationship left me deeply stressed. Finally I had to dissolve our partnership. And then in 2002 I was diagnosed with thyroid cancer and chronic lymphocytic leukemia, a disease that can be either super benign or very aggressive. (Mine was aggressive.)

My first reaction to my being sick was fear and sadness, and then later I felt great gratitude, for my illness gave me the opportunity to change my lifestyle and begin looking into my deeper self. I really believe my body had picked up the spiritual/emotional imbalances in my life, and that the path I had been on had contributed to the onset of my illness. I began to realize how important it was to be in healthy, nurturing relationships, many of which I had neglected when I was working so hard in real estate and coping with a distressing partnership.

Back then other unusual things happened, but I didn't attribute any spiritual significance to them. On our first day in a new home during my real estate sales days, a big furry coyote appeared outside our breakfast room window, stared at us for a long time, and then went away. Later on a wintry day at Tahoe, two coyotes stopped outside our newly rebuilt home and gazed through the glass French doors at me. At the time, I had no insight into either visitation. Now, however, thanks to my recent opening up to embrace my spiritual journey, I have learned that coyotes as animal guides represent transformation, leading you towards integrating your light and dark sides.

On a recent hike with my husband and daughter and her children, we 'happened' on another beautiful coyote that looked intensely at us, then wandered off. Now armed with deeper understandings, I smiled, knowing this animal is here to remind me to continue on my spiritual path.

Two months ago I was at a retreat doing a guided meditation. I had been guided to pass through a lush meadow and ascend a mountain, when suddenly a beautiful being with soft, flowing hair and garb came towards me. Intuiting immediately this angelic being was my spiritual guide, I have had many subsequent encounters, where this angel appears to comfort and support me.

When I look back to the Laura I was before my illness, I see a woman, driven and successful in her business, on the fast track of life, working seven days a week. But my insides were a tangle of stress over business plans and clients. I had lost track of my friends, had little time to spend with my family, and no time whatsoever to even think about a spiritual life. Today I am a different person. Though I continue to cope with my illness, I am presently in remission and happier, more peaceful than I've ever been. The beauty of this world and the preciousness of my family and friends are much more evident to me. And with the help of yoga, meditation, and my angel guides, I am accessing my spiritual side, its expanding horizons pulling me deeper into my inner self and into the beautiful mysteries of life.

Laura, 65, Sacramento, CA

SOUL PAINTINGS

It was the middle of the day, I was walking to my studio, and suddenly a shaft of light came down and surrounded me. Even though it was very bright and commanding, no one around me noticed it. Instantly I became a different person; every cell in my body changed, and when I went home I could no longer relate to anything in my life. Clairvoyants call this phenomenon soul rotation.

After this happened, I had out of the body experiences, where I, as a ball of light, was floating in a blue—the most amazing color of blue I had ever seen—light that felt like pure love. I had lucid dreaming and angelic visitations. One night I heard a voice telling me she was an angel here to help me in my spiritual journey.

She also told me I was here to create paintings— "soul portraits"—that would serve as a healing, transformative tool. Since then I have painted many soul paintings, and I know they are not coming from me. They are brought in from another dimension; I am only the conduit.

A couple of years later I was painting flowers. As was my technique, I lay down some watercolor paint, and keeping my paper very wet, sprinkled salt over it. When I came back an hour later to begin my painting, there was an angel on the page. I was blown away. This was the first angel painting I did—the Angel of Guidance. Her description—and the subsequent other ones— was given by my angels. "She is here to let you know, beyond a shadow of a doubt, that you are not alone. Her loving and gentle guidance is there always, to lift your spirit up and open the doorway to her world of pink light. The light of pure love. She is always there with open arms to support you through times of loneliness and fear. Allow her to guide you to a place of safety and pure love."

My paintings begin with a meditation where I ask the most appropriate angel to come forth. Then I lay down some watercolor paint on a very wet paper and sprinkle salt over it. Then I walk away from my studio and let the paper dry. When I return, an angel has appeared on the paper. An intuitive process, sometimes it takes me a while to see where the angel is on the page. It is always a beautiful experience to bring forth one of these angels.

The second angel I painted was the Angel of the Spheres. This angel represents our choices, each one bringing us lessons and growth. Some choices may be from darkness while others are directly from the light. We grow from either one. Her message is to choose wisely, for the highest good of you and others.

Next, I painted the Angel of Truth whose message I needed to hear. She reminds us to stand up, speak up, about our truth; what we know in our hearts to be true for us. She says it is appropriate to set boundaries for ourselves. Recognizing the value of our selves as individuals leads to self-esteem. It is our God-given right to love ourselves enough to say "yes" or to say "no, that's not appropriate for me at this time." The Angel of Truth is here to show you the way to love yourself enough to let your truth shine.

After I finished, I put all three paintings away. And then years later I painted the Angel of Nature. And during a workshop I was teaching,

I received the Angel of Birth and Creation. I began selling prints and cards of these angels with their messages on the back. At a transformation conference where I had a booth, I saw a well-known psychic who heals through gazing at people. As he was looking at me, I decided to call in an angel, and right there I painted the Angel of Healing and Peace.

From this angel's hands springs the white dove of peace. Healing begins by finding peace within yourself first through self love and forgiveness. Allow this angel's gift of the white dove to enter your heart and fill your every cell with peace. Take a deep breath and allow the healing to begin. Just know that she is assisting you to cleanse and purify your emotional, mental and physical bodies. When we forgive ourselves and each other, peace is our gateway to healing. I am working on my seventh angel, Angel of Faith.

Maya, 40, Kona Village, HI

A HUGE SPIRIT

When my father died unexpectedly, he joined three other angels: my great aunt, my grandmother, and my close friend, Sylvia. I often feel their presence. They are my champions, my advisors, the winds at my back. Even though I am not religious, I feel spiritually protected. I know I am not alone.

My Dad had a huge spirit, so much energy and wisdom to impart. At 78, he'd done everything he could do here on earth and needed to be free to continue his work in heaven. The way I see it is he has graduated to a bigger job description. Death is not the end of a relationship. You are simply communicating in a different way, through your reflections, thoughts, and dreams. Before he died, he said, "Jeremy, I wish I'd made you stay at home and finish 12th grade."

"Dad," I said. "It's been 33 years. Stop worrying."

Now I have a daughter in high school, and I can see everything from his point of view. Recently in a dream he told me how perfect it was that I have a daughter who is so much like me—and how much he loves us both. I am so grateful for his continued presence in my life.

Jeremy, 50, San Francisco, CA

FULL CIRCLE OF LOVE

In life, my mother and I had a difficult relationship. She never opened up to my older sister or to me. Perhaps she was still mourning the loss of her first husband, the love of her life, who was killed in WW II, three months after he joined up. Though she later married a wonderful man—our father—mother kept us as a distance, unable to cope with two small children, only ten months apart.

Three years after I was born, my brother arrived. Now she had her boy, and she loved him with all her heart. Ten years later another sister came along, who was also welcomed with open arms.

While I was growing up, I don't recall my mother showing any interest in my life. When she died, my older sister and I didn't shed a tear; my two younger siblings were devastated.

On the day of her funeral, the first two pews were reserved for immediate family, but by the time I got there, they were filled. I ended up sitting further back with my husband and children, thinking "Mother really didn't love me, and there's not even room for me in this family."

Over the next four years my mother's spirit tried many times to communicate, but I firmly shut her out. At a Deepak Chopra seminar, I was lying down at the end of a yoga session, feeling peaceful and relaxed. When I envisioned a bright red circle on my forehead, I knew mother was trying to reach me. Angrily,

I told her to go away, thinking, "Don't ruin *this* for me, Mom." At another session, the teacher played a song with the lyrics, "I've loved you for thousand years. I will love you a thousand more." I felt her presence once more. Again, I asked her to leave, unwilling to have anything to do with her.

A year later, I attended an Empowering Women Seminar. A participant broke down and sobbed, explaining that her mother had just died. Afterwards, I approached her and said, "Your tears are telling me how much you loved your mother. Celebrate this love, be grateful for it, and be comforted."

The next day, this woman told me I had helped her cope with her mother's death. *Coincidently* her mother and I shared the same name (Jane, or Janie), and the same passion (making jewelry). In gratitude, the woman gave me a bracelet her mother had designed. I knew once again that my mother was trying to communicate with me. Finally, all the pieces came together, and I realized I needed to make peace with her or I would never be emotionally whole.

Soon thereafter I was taking a walk, and felt her nearby. "Mother, I'm going to give you a chance," I said. "I'm going to let you into my heart. If you can help me bring love to this world, I'll forgive you."

This encounter changed everything. My negative feelings disappeared; I no longer felt as if I were an unloved child. Instead I knew beyond a doubt that my mother deeply loved me. Because of that I am a different person now, less judgmental of my friends, more open-hearted and compassionate. Today I work regularly at the Deepak Chopra Center, partaking in the life of the spirit.

When my father passed, we buried him at our family cabin at a lake in Wisconsin. As my sister and I walked onto the pier, we saw two eagles that would normally be searching for food in the far distance. Instead they flew directly towards us, then circled and circled, as if in a dance of love. Since then Dad has come through to me in the guise of an eagle.

Recently, I worked with a shaman who guided me through the veil that separates us from those on the other side. In this vision, an eagle appeared. I got on his back, and we flew above the treetops. Off to one side, I noticed a magnificent display of pure beautiful dancing energy. Instantly I knew it was my mother. I heard my father's voice say, "Now can you see why I loved her?"

"Yes," I answered, my heart full, "Yes, I can."

Jane, 66, Sonoma, CA

VIBRANT BRAINS

One day while walking down Sacramento Street and deep in conversation with a close friend, I felt something brush against me. Stopping in the middle of a sentence, I looked up to see a storefront sign that intrigued me: Vibrant Brains! I grabbed my friend Mary's hand, and we ran over to take a look.

We met the owners, two very bright and energetic women, committed to raising consciousness about brain fitness, who believed that regular exercise for our brains is just as important as it is for our bodies. They explained that mental workouts emphasizing reasoning, memory, language, quantitative, visual and spatial skills are tools that improve the quality of our lives. We signed up that day for their program; soon we were deep into brain plasticity.

I had no idea that this was going to be such a life-changing experience. Six months later I was on the front page of the *Wall Street Journal* in an article on "Working out at the Brain Gym."

"Linda Hale Bucklin credits a computer 'visual processing' program for helping her find her car keys faster and sharpen her tennis skills." I also didn't realize this course was going to give me a scientific explanation for our direct line to God.

I learned the world of science supports the idea of viewing the brain as two complementary halves of a whole (two cerebral hemispheres—

the left side and the right), rather than viewed as two individual ones. Lawyers, scientists, engineers, PhDs, are for the most part left-brain thinking types. Right-brain types operate differently, through their intuition and feelings.

Scientists are now giving credence to the spirituality of our brains, to the intuitive world of angel thoughts that inspires us to look beyond our rational perimeters and analytical yardsticks to another world beyond.

My work at Vibrant Brains validated all my spiritual experiences—like being able to feel my mother's presence, recognizing that friends can be angels, and that loved ones who have passed can communicate with us in many ways. I know an angel directed me through this door.

LB

NO LEAKS

Some three or four months ago, I was in the mall shopping for a forthcoming trip to our summer home in the Sierra Nevada Mountains. I had been preparing for this trip for a while for several important reasons: Issues with the house roof, some scheduled plumbing repairs, but more importantly, I wanted solitude time for me because it was my firm intention to spend the week trying to finish another part of my book.

As I was driving out of the mall's parking lot, I suddenly had to make a sharp turn to avoid an oncoming car that was going the wrong way, the exit being only one way. In doing this, I scraped the front of my car very substantially on the side of the elevation island exit.

When I got home and parked the car, I noticed a leak that seemed to be coming from the motor. I looked underneath the car, and not finding any damage, decided to depart to the mountains the next morning. Before leaving the area, I stopped at my office. Checking the car again, I noticed an oil puddle, about the same size as the one I saw the previous evening.

As my trip to the mountains would take about three hours, I grew concerned about driving the car. It was fully loaded with at least four boxes of material I needed for my book, plus a lot of other necessities. Rather despondent about the possibility of having to cancel my trip, I realized, however, I should take the car to the mechanic. Just as I was about to close the hood, a man appeared behind me and asked if I had a problem. He seemed to be just an average middle-aged man, wearing a short-sleeved shirt.

Surprised, I told him about the car problem. He asked if he could take a look. I left the hood open and he checked everything, telling me he had experience with autos. As he finished his examination, he told me there was nothing to worry about, but I still wasn't totally convinced. He noticed my anxiety and reminded me not to worry. Suddenly I felt completely reassured.

Before he departed, I thanked him very much and asked him where he lived. He pointed to the area across the road at the back of Whole Foods. I wondered where exactly, because there was only a small Senior Retirement Home for mostly disabled people on the other side of the store, but no private homes. At that moment, he said he was really rushed and had to get going. I asked him if he could come by my office some other time, as I would like to buy him coffee and thank him again. He thanked me and quickly left. I was puzzled by this kind stranger but grateful to be on my way.

Without any mishap, I arrived at our place in the Sierras. There was no indication of any further leaks. I have never seen this friendly, helpful man again. However, I had a strong feeling that our meeting was not just a happenstance, but yet another example of unexpected but very welcome help I have received from guardian angels.

Michael, 74, San Rafael, CA

ANGEL IN A WAR ZONE

I grew up in a privileged family in Latvia. My mother would travel to Paris twice a year to buy her clothes from Chanel and Dior, and we never wanted for anything–until the start of World War II. My father joined the military, and my grandmother, mother and I were suddenly on our own.

In 1944, carrying only a few possessions, we managed to escape to Germany, where we wandered from place to place. One afternoon it started to rain very hard with loud thunder and repeated bursts of lightening. Only 5, I remember running with my grandmother and mother to hide under a large tree. Out of nowhere, a farmer driving a horse-drawn cart came by and spotted us. Stopping, he scolded us for choosing such a dangerous place to take shelter.

We were shaking and very frightened of him. He turned to leave, then pulled back on the reins and motioned us to get into his cart. When we arrived at his home, his wife opened the door and was dismayed to see two filthy women and a child. But her husband insisted they take us in. We had a bed to sleep in and food for the first time in days.

We were near an area the Russians were about to take, but the man and his son led us around that, to one the Allies were controlling. The war ended soon thereafter, and we lived in a refugee camp not far from Hamburg before coming to the United States.

We are here because of a simple farmer whose heart went out to us. He could have passed by and just left us there, but instead he opened his arms and gave us shelter. We never saw him again, but his caring so deeply for us left an indelible mark on my soul. His goodness and kindness gave me the faith I hold today.

Because of him, I collect angels and at Christmas decorate our tree with angel ornaments. I know he is one of them and is still protecting us.

Ivonna, 75, Tacoma, WA

BRIDGE OF ANGELS

For me friendship is a deep commitment to showing my true self. It takes courage to reach out to a friend and lay bare my soul. I visualize a set of building blocks involving trusting, risking, trusting again, and then allowing myself to be vulnerable one more time. I think the strongest friendships evolve in this way.

When we embrace a belief in a higher power, the best of friends go to deep levels of spirituality. Together we are building a stairway to the angels, no matter how many storms and broken bridges we might encounter.

Above my desk is a picture I've had since childhood. Two children are holding hands and are about to step out onto a bridge on a wild, stormy night. The bridge crosses over a deep river gorge, and in the middle it's broken and swaying back and forth in the wind. But there is an angel guiding them, and they believe in her. Without the angel, the power of the storm might engulf the children or one might push the other one off to save herself. We absolutely need that spiritual awareness in our friendships.

Mercedes, 60, Boise, ID.

REUNITED THROUGH LOVE

For six nights, my sister and I stayed in the hospital room with my beloved father. During this entire time I hardly slept. Near the end I remember holding his hand, saying. "Dad, don't worry; you're going to see Mom again. She is waiting for you with open arms." I had a strong sense then that my parents would soon be reunited through their love.

A few hours later my father died, and I flew back to New Mexico. Beyond realizing how exhausted I was, and even though it was late and dark outside, I decided to drive the hour trip home. About 45 minutes into the trip, I must have fallen asleep. As my car was headed off the road, suddenly I felt this strong presence jolting me awake, helping me turn the wheel just in time to avoid a crash.

Right then I knew an angel was watching over me. I had a vivid feeling that someone beyond myself, perhaps even my father, was guiding me. My heart filled with gratitude, and somehow I understood at a deep level that now both my parents were protecting me, loving me as they had always done in life.

Eslee, 72, Santa Fe, NM

UNEXPECTED ANGELS

Fifteen years ago I drove my van from Alabama to Colorado to finish up a Rolfing Training Course. As I crossed into Tennessee, midway through the trip, it began to rain. Fatigued from hours of driving, I decided to pull over under a bridge ahead and fix myself a cup of tea. Slowing down, I heard a loud voice say, "No, do not stop here. Go to the Welcome Center up ahead."

I came out, refreshed and ready to continue my journey, but my van wouldn't start. The security man tried to help, with no success, and so soaking wet, I waited for the tow truck. I was relieved I hadn't pulled over under that bridge a few miles back.

At one point I went into the restroom, and there, seated in a wheelchair, was an older woman with her white hair tied up in a bun. She looked exactly like Ida Rolf, the founder of the type of bodywork I practiced. Ida had been confined to a wheelchair before her death.

"Young lady," this woman said, "I can see you're in trouble. Do you need anything?"

"No," I answered. "I'm OK. A tow truck is coming soon."

Then she said, "Do you need any money?"

"No," I said. "But thank you very much."

Suddenly, she left, disappearing into the pouring rain. I kept asking myself, "How random is that? Ida Rolf is gone. Did this really just happen?"

I didn't have much time to ponder the situation because the tow truck arrived, complete with a total hillbilly for a driver. As we left the Welcome Center, my car in tow, he started going on about a recent cockfight he'd seen, and I thought, 'Wow, I don't think I can handle this redneck for the four hour drive to Memphis.' At that moment the truck started vibrating, and his rear tire went flying by the window.

"Guess we'll need two tow trucks now," he said. He walked up the exit, called from the pay phone, and soon another truck arrived. This new driver had had acupuncture and other bodywork, and we engaged in lively conversation; the trip passed quickly. Then as I was waiting for my van to be fixed, I opened *Job's Body,* an anatomy book written by a Traeger bodyworker.

A man sat down next to me, and pointing to my book, asked, "Do you do bodywork?"

"Yes," I said. "I am about to get my degree in Rolfing."

"I'm a Traeger worker myself but my friend–I haven't seen him in two years — is a Rolfer."

At that moment another man walked in, and he turned out to be his long lost friend. Now the odds of two Rolfers and a Traeger practitioner coming together in an auto repair shop in Memphis are incredibly slim.

I have no explanation for these events. And I have never seen any of these people again. In retrospect, however, I feel they were all angels helping me at each step of that long journey, validating my work and encouraging me to continue on my path of healing.

Anita, 47, Napa, CA

HEART CONNECTIONS

Six months ago my husband died of congestive heart failure. He was surrounded by his family, and we told him it was "time to let go and see his parents and brother" who had passed on before him. He died peacefully, and we were grateful that he didn't have to suffer for long.

Months later, a week before my birthday, I was in the garage, sweeping up. In the exact spot where my husband used to sit and look out the open door, I saw a grease-shaped heart on the floor. I knew immediately that this was his way of letting me know he was happy and still loving me from a different dimension. Later, in his favorite spot on the front porch, I found another heart, again made from grease. Both are still there, and I am comforted by their presence.

A short time before my husband passed over, he lost his keys and never found them. The day before his service I was praying and saying, "OK, Rich, where *are* your keys?" Suddenly, I was directed to look in this random bag, filled with junk and off in the corner of my study. There at the bottom were his keys.

One morning I was due at work at 5:30 A.M. and despite a very thorough search of my purse and environs, I couldn't find my locker keys. Then I heard a voice say, "Look in your purse again." I did, and there hidden inside a Kleenex packet were my keys. I am positive Rich is up there guiding me, along with some other angels. I have a good feeling knowing that he is doing well and that I am protected, too.

Recently, I asked my daughter in law to take some pictures of me. When the pictures came back, I asked her what was wrong with her camera. In on picture, there was white all around me, and in another there was a shadow like a butterfly or fairy on the wall near me. Looking at these photos, a friend, a Reiki Master and healer of spiritual chakras said, "Esther, those are your angels around you."

Four years later, those hearts haven't faded and remain a vivid reminder that my husband is watching over me. I am convinced we all have guardian angels. We just need to ask them for their divine love and protection, and they will answer us. I talk to the Archangel Michael every day and ask for his guidance. Life is never perfect, but I am comforted knowing that everything will be as it is supposed to be. Everything will be OK.

Esther, 52, Petaluma, CA

MONTANA STORM

My close friends and I believe that angels are always watching over us, reminding us to be kind, loving and aware of the beauty and goodness in our world.

One day last summer, my best friend Maria and I were hiking. Married for over 30 years, with four children, Maria and her husband had been having some problems. I knew they were seeing a therapist, and that she was optimistic about weathering this personal storm. During our hike, she confided that her husband had just moved out, and she was devastated.

She couldn't stop crying. We stopped our hike, and I hugged her. As we looked around, we realized we were in a beautiful field of wildflowers. Without saying another word, we both lay down, head to head. Off to the west, we could see thunderheads building and hear faint rumblings, heralding the approach of a typical Montana storm. A rainbow arched over the far mountains.

As she looked upward, she said she felt strong arms holding her. Immediately she sensed there were angels by her side, comforting her, and reminding her, "Yes, there are storms in life, and yes, we will be with you."

Kay, 54, Helena, MT

ANGELS AROUND ME

Recently my mother died. In life she was reserved and emotionally remote, and I never sought out her advice or comfort. But since her death unexpected things have happened that make me certain she is helping me in ways she wasn't capable of when she was alive. I feel her angelic presence nearby and receive answers to many of my prayers. In fact, my awareness of angels in my midst has increased exponentially.

One Sunday my husband, weak from battling cancer, decided to take a ride in his Four-wheeler ATV just to get out of the house. When he left, I prayed to God and my angels to help him get peace and calm in his life, carry him through his pain and ease his mind. Then I started on my walk following his path. I came across him, and he said, "I rode out here, and suddenly I have such a sense of confidence and well-being." Now, I ask you, who could question angels and God?

The following days weren't as happy, and my husband became depressed and uneasy. I believe yet another angel entered our life just when we needed him. We were on a deserted, backcountry road returning home when we came across a hitchhiker. This was the middle of nowhere, about 15 miles away from the nearest town. He was 23 years old, very hungry and tired... and lost. We took him home, fed him, let him shower and then drove him to town to buy provisions. Then we took him to the trailhead that would lead him into the wilderness for the continuation of his journey.

At the end of his trip he emailed his parents (and copied us) to tell them he had met some "camping angels," but I know he was really *our* angel. By needing our help and comfort, he brought us joy and laughter at a time when we really needed it. He lifted up our hearts, especially when we received his email. We felt very grateful we touched his heart in a way he will always remember.

Katherine, 68, Big Sky, MT

A TRIAD OF ANGELS

From a young age I saw angels. Then they appeared to me as small, loose forms of radiant light in different colors: blue, red, gold, green, white. They didn't really have faces; they were like fairies, but without the detailed flower dresses and shoes made of leaves. Often my mother would find me out of my crib and walking around. "Honey, what are you doing?"

"Following the angels," I'd say.

Once when I was three, I remember my sister and me sitting side by side in our two single beds. Mom was making the rounds to tuck us in. When she went to our window to close it, we both yelled "No! Don't close it. You'll lock the angels out."

As I grew older, I saw wings and more defined forms. Recently, when I was finishing up a yoga session, melting down to my mat for our final resting pose, I had my most powerful experience with angels. As I lay there in a meditative, relaxed state, I opened my eyes and saw to my left a beautiful, big, pink angel. It felt warm looking in her direction. At my feet was a giant blue angel, shimmering and calm, like water reflecting light. And to my right was a green angel, vibrant and healing.

The pink and green angels touched my face, gently peeling back my skin as if they were folding back a sheet on a freshly made bed. A white light from within me shone forth. Feeling vulnerable and scared, I tilted my head towards the pink angel, who touched my cheek and put a comforting hand on my stomach. Her touch flushed my body with warmth. The blue angel breathed, reached into her chest and pulled out a blue triangle, just as bright and shimmering as she was.

Holding the triangle over her head, she asked, "Do you want this?"

"Only if you think I am ready," I answered.

"No," she said. "It doesn't work like that. You need to want it."

"I do want it."

Then she placed the blue triangle on my sternum. I felt pressure and then saw light entering my body. Waves of colors splashed over my white light, emotions running through me without attachment or reaction. I felt strong, yet vulnerable, overwhelmed with joy. Both the pink and green angel placed their hands on my head. Gently touching my face, they cradled my head and slid their hands over my body. They then began refolding my skin over my shimmering light, as if they were covering me with sand from the beach. I felt safe and wonderful and filled with grace.

"Please don't leave me," I whispered softly.

"We never have," they said.

Doreen Virtue coined the phrase "Indigo Child" to explain that certain beings are put on earth as direct vessels to angels and spirit guides. We are here to complete a specific mission to help this world be a better place, to raise awareness. I am one of these beings, and right now my calling is to speak up about dyslexia. I am not sure where else the universe will lead me.

If we listen to the voices of our spirit guides, we can all tap into our intuition. We're all part of this massive essence. I believe God is part of all of us, and I also believe that angels are some of the many guides in our life. They are here, reminding us that the closer we are to being a good person, and the closer we are to becoming who we need to be, brings us home to God.

McKenna, 22, Boston, MA

ANGELS IN OUR MIDST

I don't recall seeing angels until a few years after my daughter was born. It was at a time when I knew that Miko, my beloved, 18 year-old dog, was nearing the end of his life, and I had to decide when to put him down. One evening I put my head near his and whispered, "Please tell me when it's time for you to leave. Find a way to communicate that to me."

I awoke in the middle of the night and saw that the time on my digital clock was 3:17 and I knew then that March 17 (a few days later) was his chosen time. The evening after his death, I was in my bedroom, sleeping. I woke up, and there were literally thousands of angels in the room. I couldn't believe what I was seeing, but I knew absolutely they were angels. Their brightness vibrating like hummingbirds, they were all sorts of beautiful, intense colors— emerald green, violet, magenta, yellow and gold. It was overwhelming.

From that day on I was able to see angels and also auras of others. I attended a seminar, and behind the speaker at the podium I saw a large angel cross the stage. At times I'd feel a more masculine or feminine energy coming from these beautiful beings. It seemed as if they were a support system behind the lines, so to speak. Once I asked my daughter, then aged three, whether angels were boy or girl angels, and she answered in a tone that suggested I was *so* silly for asking, "Oh, Mommy, they're not boys or girls. They are beams of light."

One summer day I stopped at what I thought was a lemonade stand with three young children sitting beside it selling their goods. As I got closer, two boys and a girl, about four years-old, were selling rocks, twigs, and feathers for 10 cents a piece. Not a very elegant selection of items, but there was one beautiful feather that stood out boldly.

"I'll buy that one," I said.

As I was leaving, I stopped to ask if they'd like to bless the feather. Two of them, the girl and one of the boys, nodded. They came around the table and said, "Bless the feather, bless the feather, bless the feather." The other little boy, the quietest of the three, said, "I don't need to," and then mumbled something more that I could not make out. The oldest boy hushed the quiet one, and I knew something *spiritual* was going on.

On an impulse I asked, "Do you guys see angels?"

"Yes," they all said in a 'doesn't everyone?' tone of voice. "We see them everywhere."

"Do you see an angel around me now?"

Pointing to my shoulder, the quiet one shouted out, "Yes! It's the Archangel Gabriel."

When I do hands-on healing, both angels and spiritual beings (people who have crossed over) often communicate with me. The angel energy is much stronger, and their light is much brighter. For me spiritual beings feel almost as if a wind comes through me. As guides and guardians, they direct us more closely towards the Divine.

Tamara, 58, Santa Barbara, CA

EASTER

It is Easter Sunday at Grace Cathedral. As I listen to Pat Yankee sing "What a Wonderful World," a favorite song of mine and one that Louis Armstrong made famous, I remember an interview, perhaps on NPR, where Armstrong is asked when and where he was born. "New Orleans," he answers. "I was an orphan and never knew when my real birthday was. But I felt so lucky to be an American that I picked July 4th as mine." In Russia performing, Armstrong, a black man born in a time of division and prejudice, becomes an ambassador for world peace. The Russians love him; they can't get enough of his singing this poignant song about what a wonderful world we all live in.

I think back on Easters past when my three sons and I would dye eggs on the redwood porch of our ski house in the Sierras, the sun beating down on the rapidly melting snow. Whoosh, a chunk slides off the roof, but Christian, John and Nick, their heads bent in concentration, don't notice. I look over at Nick, at 4 the youngest, who is trying his hardest to copy John's egg, a multicolored masterpiece of swirls and sparkles.

Then one Easter we leave the Sierras for the ocean. We are staying in a remote resort perched on the edge of the Sea of Cortez in Baja. That Sunday we climb up a steep, dusty trail to a tiny whitewashed church set atop a cactus-filled hilltop. Bill, his solid presence reassuring me, goes first; Christian, John and Nick stay close by my side. We enter the cool interior of this simple church and sit together, our shoulders touching each other and the hard back of the wooden pew.

Swallows dart in and out through open arches that serve as windows, curtains of red bougainvillea framing their edges around brilliant blue sky beyond. The altar is made from polished wood, above which hangs a gilt-edged crucifix. We hear rustlings; the priest, in a crisp, white embroidered robe, walks in, surrounded by a group of young boys and girls from the nearby orphanage. Their clothes are thin and mended; their feet are bare. Holding hands, they stand quietly next to the priest. Then they begin to sing, their sweet, hopeful voices filling the church, and I know they are angels touching us with their grace.

Afterwards, we file out and there in the patio is a piñata. Crowding around it, the children take turns at trying to break it open. The air is filled with Spanish exclamations and excited yells. The piñata bursts, candy, presents and pesos flying everywhere, falling like fireworks, as the children, their eyes alight with happiness, rush to collect these precious gifts. Sometimes when I lose perspective of what is important and what isn't, I will conjure up the image of a copper coin falling into the hand of a laughing Mexican child and remember that day I felt surrounded by angels.

LB

HOPE IS A
THING WITH FEATHERS

My husband, Dick, and I often talked about what happens after we die. He promised he would never leave me. He would come back and somehow let me know he was by my side.

When Dick died a few months ago, a close friend shared this dream: Dick was meeting with a council of angels, and they asked what form he wanted to take when he came back to earth.

"A bird," he said, "because then I could fly back to my family and protect it."

Though I had never paid attention to birds, I

began to look and listen. At my window was a cardinal—the first I'd ever seen. He seemed insecure, as if he didn't know how to work the feeder, but he learned and came back often.

A few months later, I was scheduled to play in a golf tournament. Walking down the hall at the club, I noticed all the garbage cans had cardinals on them. "Hi Dick," I said, as my partner approached, wearing a hat with a cardinal on it. I knew my husband had come to reassure me.

I subscribe to an online prayer site, and recently found a picture of a cardinal, along with a story about parenting. Since my husband's death, I worried how our 21 year-old twins were handling this devastating event. I always looked to Dick for his wise counsel and advice. As I read this message, I realized the greatest gift parents can give their children is to set an example of loving each other, and acknowledging that children are not our property. Here was Dick, the cardinal, coming to me once again, telling me to let the twins spread their wings.

Recently I visited our summer home to plant some trees. When I arrived I was shocked that our neighbors had cut down the hedge between our properties, the place where my new friend, the cardinal, liked to hide. Sobbing, I completely lost it—until I heard his familiar 'chirp chirp' nearby. Immediately I got his message. "Come on, you can't accomplish anything being angry. Be strong. Forget the hedge. Go plant some trees."

At the nursery I chose two trees, but couldn't decide on the third. Suddenly I saw a beautiful cardinal in the branches of a dogwood. Turning to the assistant, I said, "I'll take that one, too."

Now hardly a day goes by that I don't see a cardinal. One morning, after walking our dog, I came home and found one sitting quietly on a ledge above our kitchen sink. I panicked. *What if*

I scare him and he flies into a window? Should I try to catch him in a towel? What if I injure him? All these feelings rushed through me, then the cardinal gathered himself and calmly flew out the door.

Yesterday I received a challenging email, one I knew I had to answer very carefully. I tried a few approaches. When I heard the cardinal's 'chirp', I knew I was on the right track. This beautiful red bird is now a part of my life. I know that Dick is always here with me, guiding and loving me, helping me to be strong and openhearted — and reminding me I am not alone.

Later, in my husband's dressing room, I saw a plaque with a quote from Emily Dickinson that I hadn't noticed before:

"Hope is the thing with feathers that perches in the soul and sings the song without the words and never stops at all."

Wendy, 54, Palm Beach, FL

AFTERWORD

Thinking I had completed this book, I prepared to send it off to my publisher. Then, unexpectedly, Bill, my beloved husband of 40 years, fell ill and was diagnosed with pneumonia. He developed severe complications. After two hospitalizations, we brought him home, where he died just six days later.

Our family was blindsided by the quickness of his passing. At 85, he had lived a long, full life yet was still strong and engaged. Now with his death, I was suddenly experiencing firsthand the reality that many wonderful people shared in their stories in my upcoming book about the power of love.

Maybe I should have been more prepared: Just before Bill fell ill, I had two identical dreams, warning dreams that I now understand. In both, I was with Bill who told me he was leaving me for someone else. I didn't know who it was, but felt I was up against a very strong force. Devastated, I begged him to stay, finally feeling I had him convinced. He took my hand and led me into a roiling, noisy crowd. Before I knew it, he'd pulled his hand away and disappeared. Calling and calling, I ran after him, but he was gone from my sight. I awoke, crying.

Since Bill's passing, I have felt his presence and his words guiding me. Daily I'm faced with many decisions and difficult situations. And then I hear his voice, advising me as usual, "Linda, for God's sake, you worry too much. It'll all work out," and I calm down.

In the last weeks of Bill's life, he needed an oxygen mask to breathe. Two nights after he died, I felt as if he were giving *me* pure oxygen and slept soundly for the first time in months, surrounded by his love.

One moment I am steady, and then I lose my balance. My grief comes in waves. It recedes, then returns, sharp and sudden. How can I see a full moon high in a black Montana sky or point out the Pleiades or hear a hawk cry or feel the soft wind on my cheek without Bill there with me? The realization that I can no longer share the beauty of this world with him sweeps through me.

How can I live without him? My anchor to windward, he was my sturdy guy who eyes lit up when I walked into a room, and who celebrated me wholeheartedly. He gave me back to myself. Memories of our times together come crowding over me, and I can hardly breathe. I am grateful to God and to Bill that we shared so many years together. And when I die, I know he will be waiting for me, his arms open wide, his unruly hair dark again, a wide smile on his face, perhaps tears of joy in his beautiful hazel eyes.

For his love and our legacy, I will go on living. When Christian, John or Nick reach out their arms and hold me tightly, when I hear sweet Sophia laugh or Katie perform Elton John's 'Your Song', when I watch Sam hit a home run or catch a glimpse of my two beautiful daughters-in-law waving at me from across a room, I will know Bill is by my side, a witness to this wonder.

Bill's old Labrador Meg, now 15, waits patiently for his return, lying quietly near our front door. Last summer, Bill and I went on a vacation and had to board her. For once in his life, he worried; he worried Meg would die without him by her side. I sense it won't be long now before Meg leaves us to be with Bill. I can picture them together again, Meg's head in his lap, her eyes looking up into his.

We will spread their ashes together high on the hill in Montana where Bill would always sit, Meg by his side, his father's binoculars around his neck, a bourbon nearby, and his warm hand in mine. Just as Bill did for me in this life, I will bear witness for him until we meet again. Always in my heart and on my mind, he is never far from me. Through love and the grace of God, in this journey we all will endure our own dark night and rise again to rejoice.

LB

ACKNOWLEDGEMENTS

My gratitude to the following authors for their generous contributions:

Valerie Andrews (also my talented editor)

Mary Callender

Michael Djordjevich

The Very Reverend Alan Jones

Susan Smith Jones

Mary Keil

Bob Litwin

Marilee Zelenek

And deepest thanks to all of you angels for sharing your beautiful stories. Your loving hearts help us understand the truth of our existence.

–Linda Hale Bucklin

A fourth generation San Francisco, Linda Bucklin has worked in public relations and as a freelance writer. Her articles have appeared in House & Garden, Journal of Commerce, and Nob Hill Gazette. She now lives in Mill Valley with her husband, and feels blessed to be surrounded by her three grown sons, two daughters-in-law, and three grandchildren.

With Mary Keil, she wrote *Come Rain, Come Shine* (Adams Press,1999), a book about women's friendships. More recently, she received accolades for *Beyond His Control* (ePublishing Works, 2008), a memoir about growing up in a privileged family and standing up to a domineering father (Prentis Hale). The central drama was her mother's death—a suicide occasioned by her father's affair with the socialite Denise Minnelli. Writer Dominick Dunne called *Beyond His Control* one of the great society books of our time and the *New York Post* dubbed it "a jolting new memoir." The book went on to become a *New York Times* bestseller, in paperback and ebook editions.

For many years, Linda has served as a trustee of Grace Cathedral and The Magic Theatre dedicated to presenting new American playwrights.

A nationally ranked tennis player, in 2006 Linda became #1 in the U.S. in 60s mixed doubles with her long-time partner Charlie Hoeveler. She holds five national titles. In addition to her family and friends, Linda's passions include duplicate bridge, duck hunting, fly fishing, and camping under the star-studded Montana sky.

CPSIA information can be obtained
at www.ICGtesting.com
Printed in the USA
FSOW01n0318100916
24743FS